ESSENTIALS OF W

At a time when developments in WTO law have made this field increasingly complex, this concise and non-technical introduction provides a timely and carefully considered overview of the substantive rules and institutional arrangements of the WTO. A variety of text features enables a rich understanding of the law; illustrative examples clarify important issues of the law and demonstrate the law's practical application; boxed summaries of key rulings in WTO case law highlight the interpretation of the relevant provisions and lead readers to a deep understanding of the meaning and application of legal rules; and recommendations for further reading allow readers to engage with current debates. Online resources include links to useful sources of information for work and research within the field. Co-written by a leading authority in the field, this is essential reading for anyone who wants to get to grips with this fascinating yet challenging field of law.

PETER VAN DEN BOSSCHE has been a Member of the Appellate Body of the World Trade Organization since 2009. He is professor of International Economic Law at Maastricht University, the Netherlands and visiting professor at the College of Europe, Bruges; the World Trade Institute, Berne; and the University of Barcelona. From 1997 to 2001, he was counsellor at the Appellate Body Secretariat and in 2001 served as Acting Director of the Secretariat. In the early 1990s, he worked as référendaire at the European Court of Justice. He studied law at the University of Antwerp (Lic.jur.), the University of Michigan (LL.M) and the European University Institute (PhD).

DENISE PRÉVOST is Associate Professor of International
Economic Law at Maastricht University, the Netherlands. She is also
a visiting lecturer at the China-EU School of Law, Beijing. She
engages in consultancy projects and gives capacity-building
workshops in the area of WTO law, for various national, European
and international bodies. She studied law at the University of
Pretoria (BLC *cum laude*, LL.B *cum laude*), University of South
Africa (LL.M) and Maastricht University (LL.M *summa cum
laude*, PhD).

ESSENTIALS
OF WTO LAW

PETER VAN DEN BOSSCHE
DENISE PRÉVOST

CAMBRIDGE
UNIVERSITY PRESS

CAMBRIDGE
UNIVERSITY PRESS

University Printing House, Cambridge CB2 8BS, United Kingdom

Cambridge University Press is part of the University of Cambridge.

It furthers the University's mission by disseminating knowledge in the pursuit of
education, learning and research at the highest international levels of excellence.

www.cambridge.org
Information on this title: www.cambridge.org/9781107035836

© Peter Van den Bossche, Denise Prévost 2016

First published 2016
Reprinted 2018

Printed and bound in the United Kingdom by Clays Ltd, Elcograf S.p.A.

A catalogue record for this publication is available from the British Library

Library of Congress Cataloguing in Publication data
Bossche, Peter van den, author. | Prévost, Marie Denise, 1971– author.
Essentals of WTO law / Peter van den Bossche, Denise Prevost.
Essentails of World Trade Organization law
New York : Cambridge University Press, 2016.
LCCN 2015041404 | ISBN 9781107035836 (hardback)
LCSH: World Trade Organization. | Foreign trade regulation. |
Arbitration (International law) | BISAC: LAW / International.
LCC K4610 .B675 2016 | DDC 343.08/70261–dc23
LC record available at http://lccn.loc.gov/2015041404

ISBN 978-1-107-03583-6 Hardback
ISBN 978-1-107-63893-8 Paperback

CONTENTS

CONTENTS

Figures

Tables

This book was motivated by the need for an accessible text providing a brief overview of the law of the WTO, which we both encountered in our own teaching and were alerted to by colleagues. As WTO law continues to gain in importance, its role in curricula is no longer limited to graduate programmes at law faculties. Instead, the study of WTO law is increasingly an integral part of graduate programmes at other faculties, undergraduate law programmes, summer schools and training programmes for government officials and other professionals. While teachers and students of graduate courses on WTO law have a choice of many excellent textbooks, providing a detailed examination of this increasingly complex area of law, the specific needs of teachers and students of undergraduate courses and courses outside the law faculty are less well served.

This book aims to fill this gap by providing a succinct introduction to the main aspects of WTO law. It provides a systematic, carefully considered discussion of the legal framework, incorporating key clarifications from the case law, that is sufficient to give the reader a strong foundation in the main aspects of WTO law. For a detailed discussion of WTO law, we refer the reader to Peter Van den Bossche and Werner Zdouc, *The Law and Policy of the World Trade Organization*, 3rd edition (Cambridge University Press, 2013).

We have drawn on many years of experience in teaching WTO law to a wide variety of audiences to write a text that aims both to stimulate the interest of students in the field of WTO law and to facilitate their learning process. To this end, this book includes fictional illustrative examples where useful to clarify key concepts and important issues and show their practical application. Recommendations for further reading complement the text and enable students to gain a more in-depth understanding of current debates and critical analysis of the issues discussed in the book. An online resources section provides students with the tools they need to work within this field.

This book reflects the current state of WTO law (as of 1 December 2015). Although we mention legal issues still to be adjudicated, we do not express in this book any opinion on how these issues should be decided or, more broadly, how WTO law should develop in the future. Where we refer to various and often divergent opinions of academics or other eminent experts in our recommendations for further reading, we do so in order to give the reader a full picture of open debates and the ongoing critical discussion of the legal issues covered in this book.

It is evident that the description of the current state of WTO law contained in this book is to be attributed to the authors in their private capacity and does not represent the views of the WTO or the WTO Appellate Body.

Peter Van den Bossche, Geneva
Denise Prévost, Maastricht

ACP	African, Caribbean and Pacific
ACWL	Advisory Centre on WTO Law
AFTA	Association of Southeast Asian Nations Free Trade Area
AMS	Aggregate measurement of support
Anti-dumping Agreement	Agreement on Implementation of Article VI of the General Agreement on Tariffs and Trade 1994
ASEAN	Association of Southeast Asian Nations
Berne Convention	Berne Convention for the Protection of Literary and Artistic Works of 1971
BoP Committee	Committee on Balance-of-Payments Restrictions
CARICOM	Common Market of the Caribbean
Code of Good Practice	Code of Good Practice for the Preparation, Adoption and Application of Standards
COMESA	Common Market of Eastern and Southern Africa

xi

CITES	Convention on International Trade in Endangered Species
CTG	Council for Trade in Goods
CTS	Council for Trade in Services
Customs Valuation Agreement	Agreement on the Implementation of Article VII of the GATT 1994
DSB	Dispute Settlement Body
DSU	Understanding on Rules and Procedures Governing the Settlement of Disputes
EC	European Communities or European Community
Enabling Clause	Decision of the GATT Contracting Parties of 28 November 1979 on Differential and More Favourable Treatment, Reciprocity and Fuller Participation of Developing Countries
EU	European Union
GATS	General Agreement on Trade in Services
GATT	General Agreement on Tariffs and Trade
GDP	Gross domestic product
GIs	Geographical indications
Goods Schedule	Schedule of Concessions
GSP	Generalized System of Preferences

Harmonized System   see HS
HS   International Convention on the
                           Harmonized Commodity
                           Description and Coding System
ICJ   International Court of Justice
IMF   International Monetary Fund
Import Licensing   Agreement on Import Licensing
Agreement   Procedures
IP   Intellectual property
IPIC Treaty   Treaty on Intellectual Property
                           in respect of Integrated Circuits
                           of 1989
ITLOS   International Tribunal on the
                           Law of the Sea
LDC   Least-developed country
MERCOSUR   Southern Common Market
MFN   Most-favoured-nation
NAFTA   North American Free Trade
                           Agreement
NAMA   Non-agricultural market access
NGO   Non-governmental organization
Paris Convention   Paris Convention for the
                           Protection of Industrial Property
                           of 1967
PPM   Process and production method
PTAs   Preferential trade agreements
Rome Convention   International Convention for the
                           Protection of Performers,
                           Producers of Phonograms and

TRIPS Agreement	Agreement on Trade-Related Aspects of Intellectual Property Rights
TRIPS Council	Council for Trade-Related Aspects of Intellectual Property Rights
TTIP	Transatlantic Trade and Investment Partnership
UN	United Nations
UN CPC	United Nations Central Product Classification
UNCTAD	United Nations Conference on Trade and Development
Understanding on BoP Provisions	Understanding on the Balance of Payments Provisions of the GATT 1994
US	United States of America
VAT	Value-added tax
VCLT	Vienna Convention on the Law of Treaties
WCO	World Customs Organization
WHO	World Health Organization
WIPO	World Intellectual Property Organization
WTO	World Trade Organization
WTO Agreement	Marrakesh Agreement Establishing the World Trade Organization

Short title	Full case title and citation
Australia – Apples (2010), 195	Appellate Body Report, *Australia – Measures Affecting the Importation of Apples from New Zealand*, WT/DS367/AB/R, adopted 17 December 2010, DSR 2010:V, 2175
Australia – Salmon (Article 21.5 – Canada) (2000), 200	Panel Report, *Australia – Measures Affecting Importation of Salmon – Recourse to Article 21.5 of the DSU by Canada*, WT/DS18/RW, adopted 20 March 2000, DSR 2000:IV, 2031
Brazil – Retreaded Tyres (2007), 93, 259	Panel Report, *Brazil – Measures Affecting Imports of Retreaded Tyres*, WT/DS332/R, adopted 17 December 2007, as modified by Appellate Body Report WT/DS332/AB/R, DSR 2007:V, 1649
Canada – Continued Suspension (2008), 204	Appellate Body Report, *Canada – Continued Suspension of Obligations in the EC – Hormones Dispute*, WT/DS321/AB/R, adopted 14 November 2008, DSR 2008:XIV, 5373
Chile – Alcoholic Beverages (2000), 35, 37	Appellate Body Report, *Chile – Taxes on Alcoholic Beverages*, WT/DS87/AB/R, WT/DS110/AB/R, adopted 12 January 2000, DSR 2000:I, 281 Panel Report, *Chile – Taxes on Alcoholic Beverages*, WT/DS87/R, WT/DS110/R, adopted 12 January 2000, as modified by Appellate Body Report WT/DS87/AB/R, WT/DS110/AB/R, DSR 2000:I, 303
China – Auto Parts (2009), 55	Appellate Body Reports, *China – Measures Affecting Imports of Automobile Parts*, WT/DS339/AB/R, WT/DS340/AB/R, WT/DS342/AB/R, adopted 12 January 2009, DSR 2009:I, 3

Chapter 1

International trade and the law of the WTO

1.1 The need for international rules on international trade

The economic prosperity of many countries largely depends on international trade. In the period 2012–2014, for example, 81 per cent of the gross domestic product (GDP) of Zambia, 63 per cent of the GDP of South Africa and 46 per cent of the GDP of Indonesia depended on international trade in goods. The increasing prosperity of China and India is without doubt largely the result of the explosive increase in their exports. There is broad consensus among economists and policymakers that economic globalization, in general, and international trade, in particular, offer an unprecedented *opportunity* to stimulate economic development and significantly reduce poverty worldwide.

> As UN Secretary General Ban Ki-moon said at the 2014 WTO Public Forum on *Why Trade Matters to Everyone*:
>
> > The question is not whether trade matters, but how we can make trade a better driver of equitable, sustainable development. How can we make trade the foundation of a life of dignity for all?... International trade is an essential component of an integrated effort

> to end poverty, ensure food security and promote
> economic growth. An ounce of trade can be worth a
> pound of aid ... Trade can – and should – benefit
> everyone. That is why the international community
> needs to avoid protectionism ... If managed well,
> international trade can be a key driver of sustainable
> development.

However, to ensure that this potential is realized, international trade has to be managed and regulated at the international level. If not, economic globalization and international trade are likely to aggravate economic inequality, social injustice, environmental degradation and cultural homogenization instead of improving the current situation.

Developed as well as developing countries need international rules on trade in order to:

- prevent trade-restrictive measures in situations where they are neither necessary nor desirable yet are imposed due to pressure from well-organized interest groups;
- give security and predictability to traders with regard to the national rules that apply to international trade in their products or services;
- ensure that important societal values and interests, such as public health, the environment, consumer safety, minimum labour standards, economic development and public morals, can be adequately protected and promoted; and
- ensure a greater measure of equity in international economic relations by providing disciplines that bind economically powerful and economically weaker countries alike,

enabling the latter to enjoy a fair share of the benefits of international trade.

> Between the strong and the weak, between the rich and the poor ... it is freedom which oppresses and the law which sets free.
>
> Abbé Jean-Baptiste Lacordaire (1802–61)

1.2 International trade law: bilateral, regional and multilateral agreements

The legal rules governing trade relations between countries are part of international economic law. International trade law (i.e. international rules on trade in goods and services) forms, together with international investment law, the 'hard core' of international economic law. This field of law consists of:

- bilateral trade agreements;
- regional trade agreements; and
- multilateral trade agreements.

There are a multitude of bilateral trade agreements, for example the Agreement on Trade in Wine between the European Union and Australia, as well as the Trade Agreement between the United States and Israel. Regional trade agreements comprise, for example, the North American Free Trade Agreement (NAFTA), a free trade area among Canada, Mexico and the United States, and the

MERCOSUR Agreement, a customs union among Argentina, Brazil, Paraguay, Uruguay and Venezuela.

The most important and broadest of all multilateral trade agreements is the Marrakesh Agreement Establishing the World Trade Organization of 1994 (commonly known as the WTO Agreement). It is the law of this Agreement – the law of the World Trade Organization (WTO) – that forms the subject matter of this introduction to international trade law. The general principles and concepts of WTO law that are set out in this introduction are, however, also applicable to a large extent to bilateral and regional trade agreements.

1.3 WTO law

The WTO was established on 1 January 1995, by the WTO Agreement.

The substantive law of the WTO can be divided into five categories:

- rules on non-discrimination;
- rules on market access;
- rules on unfair trade;
- rules on conflicts between free trade and other societal values and interests; and
- rules promoting the harmonization of national legislation in specific areas.

WTO law further consists of institutional and procedural rules, including rules on decision-making, trade policy review and dispute settlement. Together, all these substantive,

4

institutional and procedural WTO rules form the multilateral trading system.

1.4 Sources of WTO law

The principal source of WTO law is the WTO Agreement (mentioned in Section 1.3) and its multiple Annexes.

The WTO Agreement consists of only sixteen articles that concisely describe the WTO's objectives, its functions, its bodies, its membership and its decision-making procedures. However, attached to this short agreement are eighteen international agreements that form an integral part of the WTO Agreement. These agreements contain:

- multilateral agreements on trade in goods (Annex 1A), comprising:
  - the General Agreement on Tariffs and Trade 1994 (the GATT 1994) (see Sections 2.2, 2.4, 3.2, 3.3, 3.4, 3.5 4.2, 4.4, 4.5, 4.6, 4.7, 4.8, 5.2 and 5.3); and
  - initially twelve but now eleven agreements on specific aspects of trade in goods, such as:
    - the Agreement on Agriculture (see Sections 4.5.4 and 5.3.7);
    - the Agreement on the Application of Sanitary and Phytosanitary Measures (the SPS Agreement) (see Section 6.3);
    - the Agreement on Technical Barriers to Trade (the TBT Agreement) (see Section 6.2);
    - the Agreement on Implementation of Article VI of the General Agreement on Tariffs and Trade 1994 (the Anti-Dumping Agreement) (see Section 5.2);

- the Agreement on Subsidies and Countervailing Measures (the SCM Agreement) (see Section 5.3); and
- the Agreement on Safeguards (see Section 4.5);
- the General Agreement on Trade in Services (the GATS) (Annex 1B) (see Sections 2.3, 2.5, 3.6, 3.7, 4.3, 4.4, 4.6 and 4.7);
- the Agreement on Trade-Related Aspects of Intellectual Property Rights (the TRIPS Agreement) (Annex 1C) (see Section 6.4);
- the Understanding on Rules and Procedures Governing the Settlement of Disputes (the DSU) (Annex 2) (see Sections 8.1–8.8);
- the Trade Policy Review Mechanism (the TPRM) (Annex 3) (see Section 7.3.4); and
- two plurilateral agreements: one on government procurement (Section 3.5.4) and one on trade in civil aircraft (Annex 4).

The agreements in Annexes 1, 2 and 3 to the WTO Agreement are multilateral agreements and are binding on all WTO Members. Annex 4 contains two plurilateral agreements that are only binding on those WTO Members that have expressly agreed to them. The WTO Agreement comprises more than 25 000 pages, including its Annexes. Of this, 95 per cent consists of Schedules of Concessions (concerning trade in goods) and of Schedules of Specific Commitments (concerning trade in services) (see Sections 2.5, 3.2.2 and 3.6.1). In addition, the Protocols of Accession of each new WTO Member are an integral part of the WTO Agreement (see Section 7.5.2).

The WTO Agreement is not the only source of WTO law. There are other sources, but they are not of the same nature or legal status as the WTO Agreement. Most of the other sources do not, in and of themselves, provide for specific, enforceable rights or obligations. They do, however, assist in 'clarifying' or 'defining' the law that applies between WTO Members on WTO matters.

Most important among the other sources of WTO law is WTO case law (see Section 8.2). Rulings of WTO dispute settlement panels and the WTO Appellate Body are, in principle, only legally binding on the parties to the dispute in question. However, the clarifications of WTO law contained in dispute settlement reports have legal relevance beyond the dispute at issue. Especially the rulings of the Appellate Body have great authority and are, in practice, followed in later disputes on the same matter.

In *US – Stainless Steel (Mexico) (2008)* the Appellate Body held that '[e]nsuring "security and predictability" in the dispute settlement system, ... implies that, absent cogent reasons, an adjudicatory body will resolve the same legal question in the same way in a subsequent case'.

Additionally, the acts of WTO bodies, agreements concluded in the context of the WTO, customary international law and general principles of law are also recognized sources of WTO law.

> An example of an act of a WTO body is the decision of the WTO TBT Committee on Principles for the Development of International Standards, Guidelines and Recommendations. According to the Appellate Body in *US – Tuna II (Mexico) (2012)*, this decision can be considered as a 'subsequent agreement' under Article 31(3)(a) of the Vienna Convention on the Law of Treaties, and, to the extent that it 'bears specifically' on a provision of the TBT Agreement it will inform the application and interpretation of that provision.

1.5 WTO law in context

1.5.1 WTO law and international law

In the past, international trade law, and in particular GATT law (the predecessor of WTO law), was often considered to be an independent body of legal rules at the margins of international law. In the current era of economic globalization, it is uncontested that WTO law is an integral part of international law, and its role is steadily increasing in importance.

> In its very first case, *US – Gasoline (1996)*, the Appellate Body ruled that WTO law 'is not to be read in clinical isolation from public international law'.

However, the relationship between WTO rules and other rules in international law is not always clear. It is generally accepted that customary international law and general principles of law are applicable within WTO law, unless WTO law expressly contains clearly deviating rules. It is also generally accepted that international law plays an important role in the interpretation of the provisions of WTO law. WTO rules should, if possible, be interpreted in such a way that they do not conflict with other rules of international law.

In *US – Shrimp* (1998), the Appellate Body took into account multilateral environmental agreements, including the Convention on Biological Diversity and the Convention on International Trade in Endangered Species (CITES), in interpreting the exception for measures relating to the conservation of 'exhaustible natural resources' in Article XX(g) of the GATT 1994. Relying on these international agreements, the Appellate Body found that the term 'exhaustible natural resources' includes both living and non-living resources, and thus that the United States could invoke this exception to justify its regulation that aimed at the protection of sea turtles.

Nevertheless, it cannot be excluded that a conflict exists between WTO law and other international law that cannot be resolved through interpretation. In such cases, the question arises whether provisions of international agreements on the environment, human rights or minimum labour standards can be relied upon in trade disputes as justifications for violations of WTO obligations.

9

This issue is subject to much academic debate. Some scholars argue that WTO Members that are parties to a specific non-WTO agreement can invoke its rules in a WTO dispute between them as a defence against a claim of violation of WTO rules. This position is controversial and strongly contested by other WTO scholars, who point out that, as explicitly stated in Article 3.2 of the Dispute Settlement Understanding (DSU), the WTO dispute settlement system 'serves to preserve the rights and obligations of Members under the covered [WTO] agreements, and to clarify the existing provisions of those agreements'. WTO dispute settlement panels and the WTO Appellate Body may not 'add to or diminish the rights and obligations' of WTO Members as set out in the WTO agreements (see Section 8.2).

> In *Mexico – Taxes on Soft Drinks (2006)*, the Appellate Body found that there is 'no basis in the DSU for panels and the Appellate Body to adjudicate non-WTO disputes'.

It is important to note that, to date, a situation of an irreconcilable conflict between an obligation or right under a WTO agreement and an obligation or right under a non-WTO agreement has not yet arisen in WTO dispute settlement.

1.5.2 *WTO law in the European and national legal orders*

With regard to the relationship between WTO law and the national law of WTO Members, Article XVI:4 of the WTO

Agreement obliges WTO Members to ensure that their national laws are consistent with WTO law. National law, including constitutional law, may not be relied upon to justify a violation of WTO obligations.

Producers of chocolate bars in Industria, a WTO Member, are negatively affected by Industria's ban on cocoa beans that have not been certified as 'slavery free' because the complex and expensive certification process means that they can now only source their cocoa bean inputs from a restricted number of suppliers and at much higher prices. They would like to bring a case before their national courts challenging Industria's ban on cocoa beans that have not been certified as 'slavery free' on the grounds that this ban violates WTO law.

The WTO Agreement does not specify what legal effect WTO provisions are to have in the domestic legal order of WTO Members. It is left up to Members to decide whether national legislation or governmental measures can be challenged in national courts on grounds of WTO inconsistency. Most WTO Members do not allow WTO law to be directly invoked in disputes before their national courts. In other words, WTO law has no *direct effect* in the national legal orders of most WTO Members. The European Court of Justice has repeatedly refused to grant direct effect to WTO provisions. The Court referred in this context to the specific nature of the WTO dispute settlement system (see Sections 8.1–8.8) and to the fact that the most important trading partners of the European Union also do not grant direct effect to WTO law. Only in exceptional cases is direct effect given to WTO law, for example, when European Union legislation explicitly refers to WTO provisions. Also in the United States, Japan, Brazil, China and India, no direct effect is given to WTO law. By contrast, WTO law has direct effect in Mexico.

Further reading

Mavroidis, P. (2008) 'No outsourcing of law? WTO law as practiced by WTO courts', *American Journal of International Law* 421–474.

Pauwelyn, J. and Michaels R. (2012) 'Conflict of norms or conflict of laws? Different techniques in the fragmentation of public international law', *Duke Journal of Comparative and International Law* 22, 349–376.

Ruiz Fabri, H. (2014) 'Is there a case – legally and politically – for direct effect of WTO obligations?' *European Journal of International Law* 25(1), 151–173.

Sykes, K. (2014) 'Sealing animal welfare into the GATT exceptions: the international dimension of animal welfare in WTO disputes', *World Trade Review* 13(3) 471–498.

World Bank Group and World Trade Organization (2015) *The role of trade in ending poverty*, World Trade Organization, available at: www.worldbank.org/en/topic/trade/publication/the-role-of-trade-in-ending-poverty

World Trade Report (2013) *Factors shaping the future of world trade*, World Trade Organization, available at: www.wto.org/english/res_e/booksp_e/world_trade_report13_e.pdf

Chapter 2

Rules on non-discrimination

2.1 Prohibition of discrimination

The prohibition of discrimination is a key concept in WTO law and is often the subject of trade disputes between WTO Members. This prohibition finds expression in two obligations:

- the most-favoured-nation (MFN) treatment obligation; and
- the national treatment obligation.

In simple terms, the MFN treatment obligation prohibits discrimination among goods, services or service suppliers of different foreign origins (or with different foreign destinations).

> The MFN treatment obligation entails that Agricola, a WTO Member, may not grant more favourable treatment to smartphones from Industria than to smartphones from Alpinia, or treat Alpinian doctors less favourably than Industrian doctors.

The national treatment obligation prohibits discrimination between foreign goods, services and service suppliers and domestic goods, services and service suppliers.

> Under the national treatment obligation, WTO Member Agricola may not treat chocolate from Industria less

favourably than it treats its domestic chocolate, once the chocolate from Industria has entered the Agricolan market. Neither may Agricola treat Industrian coffeehouses established in Agricola less favourably than Agricolan coffeehouses.

The most important non-discrimination rules in the WTO Agreement are:

- Article I of the GATT 1994 (MFN treatment obligation for trade in goods);
- Article III of the GATT 1994 (national treatment obligation for trade in goods);
- Article II of the GATS (MFN treatment obligation for trade in services); and
- Article XVII of the GATS (national treatment obligation for trade in services).

The WTO Agreement also contains other non-discrimination provisions, such as Articles 3 and 4 of the TRIPS Agreement concerning the MFN treatment obligation and national treatment obligation for the protection of intellectual property rights. These provisions will not be discussed further in this short overview of the prohibition on discrimination in WTO law.

2.2 The MFN treatment obligation concerning trade in goods

Article I:1 of the GATT 1994 contains the MFN treatment obligation concerning trade in goods. The principal purpose of the MFN treatment obligation of this Article is to ensure all WTO Members *equality of opportunity* to export to or import from other WTO Members.

> In *EC – Seal Products (2014)*, the Appellate Body ruled that Article I is 'concerned, fundamentally, with prohibiting discriminatory measures by requiring . . . equality of competitive opportunities for like imported products from all Members' and that, for that reason, Article I does not 'require a demonstration of the *actual* trade effects of a specific measure'.

According to WTO case law, the prohibition on discrimination in Article I:1 of the GATT 1994 covers de jure as well as de facto discrimination. Therefore, not only measures that expressly refer to the national origin or destination of products are prohibited, but also measures that have the impact, in practice, of treating a product originating in, or destined for, one WTO Member less favourably than the 'like' product originating in or destined for any other country.

> If Agricola imposes a customs duty of 10 per cent *ad valorem* on chocolate from Alpinia while imposing a customs duty of 20 per cent *ad valorem* on chocolate from other WTO Members, the imposition of the 20 per cent customs duty on other WTO Members constitutes de jure discrimination or discrimination 'in law'. If, instead, Agricola imposes a customs duty of 10 per cent *ad valorem* on chocolate made with milk from cows that spend at least

six months per year at an altitude of more than 1500 metres, while imposing a customs duty of 20 per cent *ad valorem* on chocolate made with other milk, the imposition of the 20 per cent customs duty may well constitute de facto discrimination or discrimination 'in fact'. This would be so if, in fact, in Alpinia, cows spend at least six months per year at an altitude of more than 1500 metres, while the highest point in Industria, a major chocolate producer and exporter, is 300 metres above sea level.

To determine whether a measure imposed by a WTO Member is consistent with the MFN treatment obligation of Article I:1 of the GATT 1994, four questions must be answered:

- Is the measure at issue of the kind covered by Article I:1?
- Does the measure at issue confer a trade 'advantage'?
- Are the relevant products 'like products'?
- Is the advantage at issue granted 'immediately and unconditionally' to all like products concerned?

Each element of this four-step test will be discussed next.

2.2.1 *Measure covered by Article I:1 of the GATT 1994*

The first question that arises when testing for consistency with Article I:1 is whether the measure at issue is covered by this Article. Article I:1 sets out a broad range of measures that fall within its scope of application, which covers both border measures and internal measures. The *border measures* include, in particular, customs duties, other charges on imports and exports, import and export prohibitions and quotas, tariff quotas, import licences and customs formalities. The *internal measures* include, in particular, internal taxes on products and internal regulations affecting the sale, distribution or use of products. Generally, there has been little debate about the kind of measures covered by Article I:1. Both panels and the Appellate Body have recognized that Article I:1 covers a broad range of measures.

2.2.2 'Advantage'

The second question that arises when testing for consistency with the MFN treatment obligation of Article I:1 of the GATT 1994 is whether the measure at issue grants an 'advantage'. Article I:1 refers to 'any advantage, favour, privilege or immunity granted by any [Member]'. In light of the use of the word 'any', it is not surprising that the term 'advantage' has been given a broad meaning in the case law and has, so far, rarely been cause for dispute.

If Agricola lowers the customs duties on Alpinian chocolate from 20 per cent to 10 per cent *ad valorem*, it must also decrease the customs duties on chocolate from Industria (and all other WTO Members) to 10 per cent *ad valorem*. If Agricola exempts Alpinian chocolates from its prohibition on the sale of sweets in school cafeterias on its territory, it must extend this exemption to chocolates from Industria (and all other WTO Members).

2.2.3 'Like products'

By contrast, the third question, namely whether the products at issue are 'like products', is often contentious. A violation of the MFN treatment obligation can occur only when the products in question are 'like products'.

The concept of 'like products' is not only used in Article I:1 of the GATT 1994, but also in Articles III:2 and III:4 of the GATT 1994, which are discussed in Section 2.4. Although the concept of 'like products' is key to the application of the non-discrimination provisions of the GATT 1994, the GATT 1994 does not provide a definition of this concept. WTO case law on 'like products' has clarified the concept through the years and established that the scope of this concept may differ depending on the context in which it is used.

> As held by the Appellate Body in *Japan – Alcoholic Beverages II (1996)*, '[t]he accordion of "likeness" stretches and squeezes in different places as different provisions of the *WTO Agreement* are applied. The width of the accordion in any one of those places must be determined by the particular provision in which the term "like" is encountered as well as by the context and the circumstances that prevail in any given case to which that provision may apply'.

In all cases, the determination of whether products are 'like products' is, fundamentally, a determination about the nature and extent of the competitive relationship between and among those products in a particular market.

> Whereas white chocolate and dark chocolate may be 'like products' for purposes of Article III:4, they will not necessarily be 'like' in terms of Article III:2 or Article I:1 of the GATT 1994. Also, whereas white chocolate and dark chocolate may be 'like products' on the Agricolan market for purposes of Articles I:1, II:2 or III:4, they will not necessarily be 'like' in terms of these provisions on the Industrian market.

Factors that are taken into account to determine the nature and extent of the competitive relationship between and among products are, among others:

- the physical characteristics of the products;
- consumer tastes and habits regarding the products;
- the end use of the products; and
- the tariff classification of the products.

Whether the products in question are 'like' in a particular market is established on a case-by-case basis, taking into account these and all other relevant factors.

> A question that could arise in the context of Article I:1 of the GATT 1994 is whether smartphones with touchscreens and smartphones with keypads can be considered 'like products' on the Agricolan market. If they are 'like products', then any advantage given to

Alpinian touchscreen smartphones by Agricola must also be given to Industrian smartphones with keypads. By examining their physical characteristics, consumer tastes and habits, their end use, their tariff classification and other relevant factors, it will be established whether the nature and extent of the competitive relationship between these two types of smartphones is such that these products can be considered 'like' for purposes of Article I:1 of the GATT 1994.

Determining whether products are 'like' is often a difficult and controversial exercise. However, according to well-established case law, when the *only* factor distinguishing between the products at issue is their origin, it can be presumed that the products are 'like'.

A contentious issue is whether a product's process and production method (PPM) is relevant in determining whether products are 'like' if the PPM does not affect the physical characteristics of the product. Current WTO case law has been read to suggest that non–product-related PPMs are relevant in determining whether products are like when these PPMs affect consumer tastes and habits and thus affect the competitive relationship between the products concerned.

Under Article I:1 of the GATT 1994, Industria may not treat Agricolan chocolate made with cacao harvested by children less favourably than Alpinian chocolate made with cacao harvested in accordance with standards prohibiting child labour *except* if Agricolan and Alpinian chocolate are not 'like products'. Agricolan and Alpinian chocolate may not be 'like products' if the use of child labour affects the tastes and habits of Industrian consumers and thus reduces the competitive relationship between Agricolan and Alpinian chocolate in Industria's market.

2.2.4 'Immediately and unconditionally'

Finally, the question arises whether any advantage granted by a WTO Member to products originating in or destined for a particular country has been granted 'immediately and unconditionally' to all 'like products' originating in or destined for all WTO Members. 'Immediately' requires that a WTO Member not delay the granting of an advantage to all other WTO Members. 'Unconditionally' requires that a WTO Member not impose conditions that affect the equality of opportunity to import from or export to other WTO Members.

'Unconditionally' has been clarified by the Appellate Body in EC – Seal Products (2014). Pointing to the aim of Article I:1 of protecting expectations of equal competitive opportunities for like imported products from all Members, it noted that Article I:1 does not prohibit a Member from attaching any conditions to the granting of an 'advantage'. 'Instead, it prohibits those conditions that have a detrimental impact on the competitive opportunities for like imported products from any Member'.

2.2.5 *An obligation with many exceptions*

Although the MFN treatment obligation is a fundamental principle of WTO law, it should be noted that there is, in practice, an increasing number of arrangements that deviate from this obligation and which grant products from some WTO Members more favourable treatment than is granted to 'like products' from other Members. Examples of such arrangements are the preferential treatment of developing countries and agreements that establish a free-trade area or a customs union. Exceptions to the MFN treatment obligation that are in conformity with WTO law will be discussed in Sections 4.2–4.4 and 4.7–4.8.

2.3 The MFN treatment obligation concerning trade in services

Article II:1 of the GATS contains the MFN treatment obligation concerning trade in services. The main purpose of the MFN treatment obligation of Article II:1 of the GATS is to ensure all WTO Members *equality of opportunity* to supply services, regardless of the origin or destination of the services or the nationality of the service suppliers.

The prohibition of discrimination in Article II:1 of the GATS covers de jure as well as de facto discrimination.

Agricola has a vibrant café culture involving coffee brewed in earthenware pots and live folk music in traditional coffeehouses. To prevent the dilution of this cultural heritage by foreign coffeehouse chains such as

> Coffeebucks, Agricola prohibits the establishment of for-
> eign coffeehouses except for those from its neighbour
> Utopia, with which it shares this cultural heritage. Such a
> measure discriminates explicitly on the basis of the
> national origin of the service suppliers and therefore
> constitutes de jure discrimination in violation of Article
> II:1 of the GATS. If, instead, Agricola requires that all
> coffeehouses established on its territory offer coffee
> brewed in the above-mentioned traditional manner and
> provide live performances by musicians skilled in its folk
> music, it may also violate Article II:1 of the GATS.
> Although this measure does not explicitly distinguish
> between the service suppliers on the basis of national
> origin, Agricola may be discriminating de facto between
> coffeehouses from Utopia and coffeehouses from other
> WTO Members because the latter coffeehouses do not,
> or are less likely to, meet the above-mentioned
> requirements.

To determine whether a measure of a WTO Member
is inconsistent with the MFN treatment obligation of Article
II:1 of the GATS, three questions must be answered:

- Is the measure at issue covered by Article II:1?
- Are the relevant services or service suppliers 'like services'
  or 'like service suppliers'?
- Are the services or service suppliers of all WTO Members
  immediately and unconditionally accorded treatment no
  less favourable than the like services or service suppliers
  of any other country?

Each element of this three-step test will be addressed next.

2.3.1 *Measures covered by Article II:1 of the GATS*

According to Article I:1 of the GATS, this Agreement applies to 'measures by Members affecting trade in services'. The GATS does not define the term 'services', but it does state that 'services' as meant under the GATS include 'any service in any sector'. There are twelve broad services sectors (e.g. business services, communication services, distribution services, environmental services and financial services), which are further divided into 150 subsectors (the sector of communication services, for example, is divided into postal services, courier services, telecommunication services [including *inter alia* voice telephone services, electronic mail and voice mail] and audiovisual services [including *inter alia* motion picture production and distribution services, radio and television services and sound recording]). The only services not covered by the GATS are 'services supplied in the exercise of governmental authority' under Article I:3(b) of the GATS. These are defined in Article I:3(c) as services which are supplied neither on a commercial basis nor in competition with one or more service suppliers, such as police services or, at least in most WTO Members, prison services.

The GATS defines the term 'trade in services' in Article I:2 as the supply of a service through one of four defined modes of supply:

Mode 1: the cross-border mode of supply, in which the service supplier and the service recipient remain in their respective countries, but the service itself crosses the border.

An example of Mode 1 supply is the medical advice that an Industrian cardiovascular surgeon gives by telephone or through e-mail to a patient residing in Agricola.

Mode 2: the consumption abroad mode of supply, in which the service recipient travels to the service supplier's country to receive the service.

An example of this mode of supply is a patient from Agricola who travels to Industria to undergo cardiovascular surgery.

Mode 3: the commercial presence mode of supply, in which the service supplier has any type of business or professional establishment in the country of the service recipient.

Examples of this mode of supply are the establishment in Agricola of a hospital for cardiovascular surgery by a medical services company from Industria and the establishment by an Industrian cardiovascular surgeon of a practice in Agricola.

Mode 4: the presence of natural persons mode of supply, in which the service supplier temporarily moves to the country of the service recipient to provide the service.

> An example of this mode of service supply is an Industrian cardiovascular surgeon who travels to Agricola to perform a surgery.

As mentioned earlier, the GATS applies to 'measures by Members affecting trade in services'. 'Measures by Members' include measures taken by central, regional and local governments and authorities, but also measures taken by non-governmental bodies, such as bar associations or medical associations, when they exercise governmental authority delegated to them. For a measure to 'affect' trade in services, this measure is not required to regulate trade in (that is, the supply of) services. A measure affects trade in services when the measure bears upon the conditions of competition in the supply of a service, even though the measure may regulate other matters.

From the preceding discussion, it follows that the scope of application of the GATS, and of GATS obligations such as the MFN treatment obligation of Article II:1, is extremely broad. Yet, not all measures to which the GATS applies are subject to the MFN treatment obligation of Article II:1. Unlike the GATT 1994, the GATS allows Members *to exempt* measures from the MFN treatment obligation. Pursuant to Article II:2 of the GATS, a WTO Member may maintain a measure inconsistent with the MFN treatment obligation of Article II:1 provided that it listed such measure in the Annex on Article II Exemptions before the date of entry into force of the WTO Agreement. The list of exempted measures of each Member can be found on the WTO website.

> Agricola could, for example, have exempted its measures for the protection of its traditional café culture from the application of the MFN treatment obligation so that more favourable treatment could be granted to Utopian coffeehouses than to coffeehouses from Industria and other WTO Members with which it does not share this common cultural heritage.

2.3.2   *'Like services' and 'like service suppliers'*

Similar to the term 'like products', 'like services' and 'like service suppliers' are essential but problematic terms in the context of the MFN treatment obligation of Article II:1 of the GATS. A violation of the MFN treatment obligation can occur only when the 'services' or 'service suppliers' in question are 'like'. However, the concepts of 'like services' and 'like service suppliers' are not defined in the GATS, and, to date, there is almost no relevant case law interpreting them in the context of Article II:1. Some early case law suggests that, to the extent that service suppliers provide 'like services', they are 'like service suppliers'. However, the question arises whether this is always the case or whether, for example, the size of the service suppliers, their assets and the nature and extent of their expertise must also be taken into account when deciding whether service suppliers providing 'like services' are 'like service suppliers'. Due to the intangible nature of services and the different modes of supply, it is clear that the terms 'like services' and 'like service suppliers' raise even more complicated conceptual questions than the term 'like products' in the GATT 1994.

Examples of such questions are whether commercial coffeehouse chains such as the Industrian Coffeebucks chain and traditional coffeehouses such as those of Utopia provide 'like services' and whether Industrian doctors who must complete five years of university studies and two years of practical training in order to qualify to practice medicine and Utopian doctors who qualify immediately after completing a five-year medical degree are 'like service suppliers'.

The case law on the concepts of 'like services' and 'like service suppliers' under the national treatment obligation contained in Article XVII of the GATS, discussed in Section 2.5.3, is probably a useful source of inspiration when answering these questions.

2.3.3 'Treatment no less favourable'

Finally, the services or service suppliers of any given WTO Member must be accorded, immediately and unconditionally, 'treatment no less favourable' than the treatment accorded to like services or service suppliers of any other country. It is generally accepted that treatment of services or service suppliers is 'less favourable' when the measure at issue alters the conditions of competition in favour of like services or service suppliers from any other country.

It thus follows that if Agricola allows Ethnica, a Utopian chain of coffeehouses, to establish branches in its cities, it is obliged, in accordance with the MFN treatment obligation, to grant this right to coffeehouse chains of all other WTO Members – including Coffeebucks from Industria – under the same conditions.

2.4 National treatment obligation concerning trade in goods

The prohibition of discrimination finds expression, aside from in the MFN treatment obligation, also in the national treatment obligation. Article III of the GATT 1994 contains the national treatment obligation concerning trade in goods. In terms of this obligation, WTO Members must treat imported products, once they have entered the domestic market, no less favourably than 'like' domestic products.

The principal purpose of the national treatment obligation of Article III is, as stated in Article III:1, to ensure that internal measures are not applied on imported or domestic products in such a way that they afford protection to domestic production. Toward this end, Article III obliges WTO Members to provide *equality of competitive conditions* for imported products in relation to domestic products.

As held by the Appellate Body in *EC – Seal Products (2014)*, Article III aims to ensure 'equality of

> competitive *opportunities* for imported products and like domestic products', and thus it does not 'require a demonstration of the *actual* trade effects of a specific measure'.

The prohibition on discrimination in Article III covers de jure as well as de facto discrimination.

> The measure at issue in *Japan – Alcoholic Beverages II (1996)* was tax legislation that imposed higher taxes on alcoholic beverages such as whisky, brandy and vodka (whether domestic or imported) than on shochu (whether domestic or imported). Although this tax legislation was 'origin-neutral' on its face, in fact, it discriminated against imported alcoholic beverages and favoured a traditional domestic alcoholic beverage.

The national treatment obligation concerns both internal taxation (Article III:2) and internal regulation (Article III:4). The national treatment obligation with regard to internal taxation is applicable to 'like products' (Article III:2, first sentence) as well as to 'directly competitive or substitutable products' (Article III:2, second sentence). Note, however, that, pursuant to Article III:8(a) and (b), the national treatment obligation of Article III does not apply to government procurement measures and direct subsidies to domestic producers.

2.4.1 *Article III:2, first sentence*

To determine whether an internal tax of a WTO Member is consistent with the national treatment obligation of Article III:2, first sentence, of the GATT 1994, three questions must be answered:

- Is the measure at issue an 'internal tax' that is directly or indirectly applied on the products in question?
- Are the imported and domestic products 'like products'?
- Are the imported products taxed 'in excess' of the domestic products?

Each element of this three-step test is discussed next.

2.4.1.1 'Internal taxes'

The taxes referred to in Article III:2 are internal taxes and other internal charges applied directly or indirectly on products. Therefore the national treatment obligation of Article III:2 does not apply to customs duties (because these are not internal charges) or to income taxes (because these are not taxes on products). A tax is applied directly on a product if it is applied on the product as such. A tax is applied indirectly when something that is related to the product, such the inputs or raw materials used in the production of the product, is taxed.

Typical examples of internal taxes in the sense of Article III:2 are value-added taxes (VAT), sales taxes and excise duties.

2.4.1.2 'Like products'

As mentioned earlier, the term 'like products' is also used in Article III:2, first sentence, of the GATT 1994. Whether imported and domestic products are 'like' must be established on a case-by-case basis by determining the nature and extent of the competitive relationship between and among the products concerned. During this determination, the factors previously discussed in Section 2.2.3 with regard to Article I:1 (physical characteristics, end use, customer tastes and preferences, and tariff classification) are examined, amongst others. According to established case law, the term 'like products' as understood in Article III:2, first sentence, must be interpreted narrowly.

> As stated by the Appellate Body in *Japan – Alcoholic Beverages II (1996)*, in respect of 'like products' in the first sentence of Article III:2, the 'accordion of "likeness" is meant to be narrowly squeezed'.

Products will only be considered 'like' under Article III:2, first sentence, if there is a strong competitive relationship between the imported and domestic products. If a broad interpretation were given to concept of 'like product' in Article III:2, first sentence, Article III:2, second sentence, which concerns directly competitive or substitutable products, would become redundant to a large extent.

> Dark chocolate and white chocolate, although they may compete sufficiently in Agricola's market to be 'like products' for purposes of Article 1:1 of the GATT 1994, may not be in a strong enough competitive relationship to be regarded as such under the narrow concept of 'like products' in Article III:2, first sentence, of the GATT 1994.

32

2.4.1.3 Taxes 'in excess of'

With respect to the requirement that the internal taxes on imported products may not be 'in excess of' the internal taxes applied to 'like' domestic products, it should be noted that, according to established case law, even the slightest additional tax on imported products is prohibited.

From Article III:2, first sentence, of the GATT 1994, it follows that Industria may not impose a VAT of 22.1 per cent on imported smartphones if the VAT on domestic smartphones is 22 per cent.

2.4.2 Article III:2, second sentence

According to Article III:2, second sentence, of the GATT 1994 (which should be read together with the Note *Ad* Article III:2), the national treatment obligation with regard to internal taxes is also applicable to directly competitive or substitutable products.

To determine whether an internal tax of a WTO Member is consistent with the national treatment obligation as set out in Article III:2, second sentence, of the GATT 1994, four questions must be answered:

- Is the measure at issue an 'internal tax' that is directly or indirectly applied on the relevant products?
- Are the imported and domestic products 'directly competitive or substitutable'?
- Are these products not similarly taxed?

- Is the dissimilar taxation applied so as to afford protection to domestic production?

Each element of this four-step test is discussed next.

2.4.2.1 'Internal taxes'

The concept of 'internal taxes' has already been discussed earlier, under Section 2.4.1.1, with regard to Article III:2, first sentence. Its meaning is the same under the second sentence of Article III:2.

2.4.2.2 'Directly competitive or substitutable products'

As is the case with the term 'like products', the term 'directly competitive or substitutable products' has not been defined in the GATT 1994. It is clear, however, that this concept is broader than the concept of 'like products' as understood in Article III:2, first sentence. Article III:2, second sentence, thus covers a broader category of products than Article III:2, first sentence. 'Like' products are a subset of directly competitive or substitutable products.

Whether imported and domestic products are 'directly competitive or substitutable products' is determined on a case-by-case basis, taking into account the factors for the determination of likeness discussed previously, as well as other factors (see Section 2.2.3). The determination primarily consists of an examination of the nature and extent of the competitive relationship between the imported and domestic products, including the price elasticity of demand for the products in question. According to the case law, products are considered to be 'directly competitive or substitutable' when they are interchangeable or when they offer alternative ways of satisfying a particular need or taste.

> In *Japan – Alcoholic Beverages II (1996)* and *Korea – Alcoholic Beverages (1999)*, the traditional domestic alcoholic beverages, shochu and soju, respectively, were found to be 'directly competitive or substitutable' with imported 'Western-style' liquors, such as whisky, vodka, brandy, cognac, rum, gin and liqueurs. In *Chile – Alcoholic Beverages (2000)*, the 'directly competitive or substitutable' products were domestically produced pisco and imported distilled spirits, such as whisky, brandy and cognac. In *Mexico – Taxes on Soft Drinks (2006)*, domestic cane sugar was regarded as 'directly competitive or substitutable' with imported high fructose corn syrup.

Both *latent* and *extant* demand must be analyzed due to the dynamic and evolving nature of competition in the marketplace and the fact that the object and purpose of Article III is to protect *expectations* of equal competitive relationships between imported and domestic products.

> For example, on Agricola's market, domestically produced dark chocolate may be *potentially* interchangeable with white chocolate imported from Agricola because the two products are alternative means of satisfying the taste of Agricolan consumers for chocolate treats. The fact that, due to the much higher VAT imposed by Agricola on white chocolate, consumers in Agricola do not *currently*

see the two products as interchangeable, is not enough to conclude that they are not 'directly competitive or substitutable' products within the meaning of Article III:2, second sentence.

2.4.2.3 'Not similarly taxed'

According to case law, the requirement of similar taxation of imported and domestic products does not imply that the same or identical taxes must be imposed on these products. Contrary to the obligation under Article III:2, first sentence, a small difference in taxes is permitted under Article III:2, second sentence.

In *Japan – Alcoholic Beverages II (1996)*, the Appellate Body explained that '[t]o interpret "in excess of" and "not similarly taxed" identically would deny any distinction between the first and second sentences of Article III:2. Thus, in any given case, there may be some amount of taxation on imported products that may well be "in excess of" the tax on domestic "like products" but may not be so much as to compel a conclusion that "directly competitive or substitutable" imported and domestic products are "not similarly taxed"'.

2.4.2.4 'So as to afford protection to domestic production'

To establish a violation of Article III:2, second sentence, it is not enough to prove dissimilar taxation of directly competitive or substitutable products. The dissimilar taxes on imported and domestic products must further be applied in such a way that domestic production is afforded protection, contrary to the principal purpose of the national treatment obligation as laid down in Article III:1 of the GATT 1994. In determining whether this is the case, the intent of the government is irrelevant.

In *Chile – Alcoholic Beverages (2000)*, Chile argued that the tax differences applicable to alcoholic beverages were aimed at reducing the consumption of alcoholic beverages with higher alcohol content. The Appellate Body did not regard the stated objectives as constituting an effective rebuttal by Chile of the alleged protective application of the internal taxation on alcoholic beverages.

Instead of examining the intent of the government, a complete and objective analysis of the design, structure and overall application of the tax measure concerned must be made to determine the existence of a protective application.

For example, if Agricola's taxes on chocolate operate in such a way that the lower tax bracket covers primarily domestically produced dark chocolate, whereas the higher tax bracket encompasses primarily imported white chocolate, the implication is that the tax measure is applied so as to afford protection to domestic production. The fact that the real or alleged intent of the Agricolan government is to discourage the consumption of white chocolate, which is known to be less healthy than dark chocolate, is irrelevant in this context (see, however, Section 6.2.2).

2.4.3 *Article III:4*

As mentioned earlier, the national treatment obligation of Article III of the GATT 1994 concerns not only internal taxation, but also internal regulation. The relevant provision is Article III:4 of the GATT 1994. To determine whether a measure is inconsistent with the national treatment obligation of Article III:4, three questions must be answered:

- Is the measure at issue a law, regulation or requirement covered by Article III:4?
- Are the imported and domestic products 'like products'?
- Are the imported products accorded less favourable treatment?

Each element of this three-step test is discussed next.

2.4.3.1 'Laws, regulations and requirements'

The measure at issue is a measure covered by Article III:4, when it is a law, regulation or requirement that affects the internal sale, offering for sale, purchase, transportation, distribution or use of products. It is clear that the scope of application of Article III:4 with respect to the national treatment obligation is broad, also because – according to well-established case law – Article III:4 does not only cover measures that govern, but also measures that have an effect on, the sale, offer for sale, purchase, transportation, distribution or use of the products. To fall within the scope of application of Article III:4, it is sufficient that a measure may modify the conditions of competition between imported and domestic products.

Examples of measures that, according to the case law, fall within the scope of the obligation of Article III:4 of the GATT 1994 are minimum price requirements for domestic and imported beer, the limitation of the number of points of sale for imported alcoholic beverages, regulations that result in higher transportation costs for imported grain, a ban on cigarette advertising, and an obligation to dispose of ten used tyres as a prerequisite for the importation of one retreaded tyre.

2.4.3.2 'Like products'

In respect of the question whether imported and domestic products are 'like products', please refer to the discussion of this term in Section 2.2.3. Once again, the determination of 'like products' involves an assessment of the nature and extent of the competitive relationship between and among the products at issue based on, among others, the physical characteristics of the products, their end use, consumer tastes and habits and the tariff classification of the products.

In *EC – Asbestos (2001)*, where the measure at issue was a French ban on chrysotile asbestos fibres and products containing chrysotile asbestos fibres, the Appellate Body considered the health risks of asbestos, a known carcinogen, as relevant under the 'physical characteristics'

> criterion as well as under the criterion of 'consumer tastes and habits'. It therefore found that chrysotile asbestos fibres and products containing chrysotile asbestos fibres were *not* 'like' PCG fibres and products containing PCG fibres, which did not have the same health risks.

According to the case law, the scope of the concept of 'like products' under Article III:4 is broader than the scope of this concept under Article III:2, first sentence. However, it is certainly not broader than the *combined* scope of the concept of 'like products' under Article III:2, first sentence, and the concept of 'directly competitive or substitutable products' under Article III:2, second sentence.

> It is possible that smartphones with touchscreens and smartphones with keypads are 'like products' in Agricola's market within the meaning of Article III:4 of the GATT 1994, whereas they are not 'like products' within the meaning of Article III:2, first sentence, of the GATT 1994. In that case, it is probable that smartphones with touchscreens and smartphones with keypads are 'directly competitive or substitutable products' under Article III:2, second sentence.

2.4.3.3 'Treatment no less favourable'

According 'treatment no less favourable' to imported products means according to these products conditions of competition no less favourable than is accorded to the like domestic products. A measure accords treatment less favourable and is thus inconsistent with Article III:4 when it modifies the *conditions of competition* in the relevant market to the detriment of imported products.

Moreover, to support a finding of treatment 'less favourable' under Article III:4, a genuine relationship between the measure at issue and its adverse impact on competitive opportunities for imported versus like domestic products is required.

> In *Korea – Various Measures on Beef (2001)*, the Appellate Body noted that: 'A formal difference in treatment between imported and like domestic products is thus neither necessary, nor sufficient, to show a violation of Article III:4. Whether or not imported products are treated "less favourably" than like domestic products should be assessed instead by examining whether a measure modifies the *conditions of competition* in the relevant market to the detriment of imported products'.

2.5 National treatment obligation concerning trade in services

The national treatment obligation for measures that affect trade in services is set out in Article XVII of the GATS. This national treatment obligation is fundamentally different in scope from the GATT national treatment obligation discussed in Section 2.4. Whereas the national treatment obligation of Article III of the GATT 1994 applies in principle to all measures affecting trade in goods, the national treatment obligation of Article XVII of the GATS applies only to measures affecting trade in services to the extent that a WTO Member has explicitly committed itself to grant 'national treatment' in respect of specific services sectors. Members set out such commitments in their 'Schedule of Specific Commitments', commonly known as their Services Schedule. These Schedules are attached to the GATS and are an integral part thereof. They can be consulted on the WTO website.

Whether a Member makes a commitment in a specific services sector depends on negotiations. Therefore, in principle, a Member is free to decide whether to make a commitment, and, even when such a commitment is made, it is often made subject to conditions and qualifications that limit the obligation's scope of application. When these limitations relate to commitments regarding specific services sectors, they are recorded in the column entitled 'Limitations to national treatment' in the sector-specific part of the Member's Services Schedule, under the relevant service sector and mode of supply. Limitations that apply generally to the national treatment commitments made in all services sectors are recorded in the first part of a Member's Services Schedule, the 'Horizontal Commitments' part.

The principal purpose of the national treatment obligation of Article XVII:1 is to ensure *equal competitive opportunities* for like services and like service suppliers of other WTO Members. As explicitly provided in Article XVII:3 of the GATS, the national treatment obligation covers both de jure and de facto discrimination.

To determine whether a measure is consistent with the national treatment obligation of Art XVII of the GATS, four questions must be answered:

- Has the Member made a commitment to provide national treatment with regard to the services sector and mode of supply at issue?
- Is the measure at issue a measure by a Member affecting trade in services?
- Are the foreign and domestic services or service suppliers at issue 'like services' or 'like service suppliers'?
- Are the foreign services or service suppliers granted 'treatment no less favourable' than domestic services or service suppliers?

Each element of this four-step test will be discussed here.

2.5.1 *National treatment commitment*

As already stated, the national treatment obligation of Article XVII:1 of the GATS does not apply generally to all measures affecting trade in services. This obligation applies only to measures affecting trade in services to the extent that a WTO Member has explicitly committed itself to grant national treatment in respect of specific services sectors. In applying Article XVII, it is therefore necessary to carefully examine a Member's Services Schedule to determine whether, and if so to what extent, a Member has committed itself to provide national treatment in the relevant services sector and mode of supply.

For example, see the following excerpt:

43

Table 2.1 *Excerpt of the Services Schedule of Industria*

I HORIZONTAL COMMITMENTS

Sector or subsector	Limitations on market access	Limitations on national treatment
All sectors included in this Schedule	(4) Unbound, except for specialists, being natural persons with essential technical or professional skills assessed in terms of the applicant's employment experience and qualifications, and the scarcity of such skills in Industria.	(3) Eligibility for subsidies may be limited to legal persons established within the national territory.

II SECTOR-SPECIFIC COMMITMENTS

Sector or subsector	Limitations on market access	Limitations on national treatment
Human health services (UN CPC 931)		
93122 Specialized medical services	(1) None (2) None (3) Subject to a maximum of thirty foreign hospitals (4) Unbound, except as indicated in the horizontal section	(1) Three years of professional practice in Industria required (2) None (3) Industrian nationality required to establish an independent practice (4) Unbound

(1) cross-border, (2) consumption abroad, (3) commercial presence, (4) natural persons

From the sector-specific part of this Services Schedule it appears that Industria has made national treatment commitments in the subsector of specialized medical services. Although it has made a full national treatment commitment (i.e. no limitations) in mode 2 (consumption abroad), it has recorded limitations in both mode 1 (cross-border supply) and mode 3 (commercial presence). Industria has made no national treatment commitments in mode 4 (movement of natural persons). In addition, in the 'Horizontal Commitments' part of its schedule, Industria has inscribed a general limitation on national treatment for all service sectors in which commitments have been made in mode 3 (commercial presence).

Because the Services Schedules of Members are an integral part of the GATS, they must be interpreted in accordance with customary international law rules on treaty interpretation, as codified in Articles 31 and 32 of the Vienna Convention on the Law of Treaties (discussed further in Section 8.2).

2.5.2 'Measure by a Member affecting trade in services'

This second element of the four-step test was already discussed in Section 2.3.1.

2.5.3 'Like services' or 'like service suppliers'

The national treatment obligation of Article XVII of the GATS applies only between 'like' services or service suppliers. Although there is no definition of these concepts in the GATS, there is now some case law clarifying them. The determination of whether services or service suppliers are 'like' under Article XVII:1 should be made case-by-case on the basis of the evidence as a whole. It has also been established that at the core of the 'likeness' analysis is the 'competitive relationship of the services being compared'.

> The panel in *China – Electronic Payment Services (2012)* held that services are 'like' for the purposes of Article XVII:1 if 'it is determined that the services in question in a particular case are essentially or generally the same in competitive terms'.

Whereas in some cases the fact that the services provided are like may 'raise a presumption' that the service suppliers are like, in other cases a separate enquiry as to the likeness of the service suppliers may be called for.

2.5.4 'Treatment no less favourable'

With regard to the last element of the four-step test, Article XVII:3 of the GATS clarifies that treatment (whether it is formally identical or formally different) is considered less favourable 'if it modifies the conditions of competition in favour of services or service suppliers of the Member concerned compared to like services or service suppliers of any other Member'.

Agricola has made a commitment to provide national treatment to 'accommodation, food and beverage services' (UN CPC 63) in its Services Schedule, with no limitations in mode 3. As discussed earlier, to prevent the dilution of its cultural heritage by foreign coffeehouse chains such as Coffeebucks, Agricola requires that *all* coffeehouses established on its territory offer coffee brewed in earthenware pots and provide live performances by musicians skilled in its folk music. To the extent that such requirements modify the conditions of competition between Agricolan coffeehouses and foreign coffeehouses to the detriment of the latter, these requirements give raise to de facto less favourable treatment inconsistent with Article XVII of the GATS.

Further reading

MFN treatment obligations

Adlung, R., and Carzaniga A. (2009) 'MFN exemptions under the General Agreement on Trade in Services: grandfathers striving for immortality'? *Journal of International Economic Law* 12(2) 357–392.

Gowa, J., and Hicks, R. (2012) 'The Most-Favored Nation rule in principle and practice: discrimination in the GATT', *Review of International Organizations* 7 247–266.

Grossman, M. G., and Sykes, O. A. (2005) 'A preference for development: the law and economics of GSP', *World Trade Review* 4 41–67.

McRae, D. (2012) 'MFN in the GATT and the WTO', *Asian Journal on WTO and International Health Law and Policy* 7(1) 1–24.

Ortino, F. (2008) 'The principle of non-discrimination and its exceptions in GATS: selected legal issues', in M. Andenas and K. Alexander (eds.), *The World Trade Organization and Trade in Services*. Leiden/Boston: Brill/Nijhof, 173–206.

Pauwelyn, J. (2009) 'Multilateralizing regionalism: what about an MFN clause in preferential trade agreements'? *Proceedings of the Annual Meeting of the American Society of International Law* 103 122–124.

National treatment obligations

Cossy, M. (2006) 'Determining "likeness" under the GATS: squaring the circle'?, in P. Sauve, M. Panizzon, N. Pohl (eds.), *Staff Working Paper* ERSD-2006-08. New York: WTO.

Davey, J. W., and Maskus, E. K. (2013) 'Thailand–Cigarettes (Philippines): A more serious role for the 'less favourable treatment' standard of Article III:4', *World Trade Review* 12 163–193.

Flett, J. (2013) 'WTO space for national regulation: requiem for a diagonal vector test' *Journal of International Economic Law* 16(1) 37–90.

Horn, H., and Mavroidis, C. P. (2004) 'Still hazy after all these years: the interpretation of national treatment in the GATT/WTO case-law on tax discrimination', *European Journal of International Law* 15 39–69.

Ming, D. (2015) '"Treatment no less favorable" and the future of national treatment obligation in GATT Article III:4 after EC–Seal Products', *World Trade Review* (published online 1 June 2015). Available at: http://journals.cambridge.org/article_S147474561 5000245

Zhou, W. (2012) 'The role of regulatory purpose under Articles III: 2 and 4 – toward consistency between negotiating history and WTO jurisprudence', *World Trade Review* 11(1) 81–118.

Chapter 3
Rules on market access

3.1 Introduction

Secure and predictable access to markets is essential for international trade. However, access for goods and services from other countries to the market of a WTO Member is frequently impeded or restricted in various ways. These restrictions can be in the form of either tariffs or non-tariff barriers to trade. The most common tariff barriers to trade are – at least for goods – customs duties. Tariff barriers to trade can also take the form of other duties and charges on imports and exports. Non-tariff barriers to market access – for goods as much as for services and service suppliers – comprise:

- quantitative restrictions, such as quotas and bans; and
- other non-tariff barriers, such as technical barriers to trade, lack of transparency of national trade regulation, unfair and arbitrary application of national trade regulation, customs formalities and procedures and government procurement practices.

Different WTO rules are applicable to these various tariff and non-tariff barriers to market access. This different treatment reflects a difference in the economic impact of these trade barriers.

49

3.2 Customs duties and other duties and charges on imports

A customs duty, or tariff, on imports is a financial charge or a tax on goods, due because of their importation. Market access for the goods concerned is conditional upon the payment of the customs duty. Most customs duties on imports are *ad valorem* (i.e. a percentage of the value of the imported product).

> For example, the customs duty of Agricola on imports of chocolate bars is 12 per cent *ad valorem*. Therefore, the importation of chocolate bars to the value of €10 000 will be subject to a customs duty of €1200.

Customs duties may also be *specific*, that is based on a unit of quantity such as weight (kg), length (m), area (m²), volume (m³ or l) or numbers (pieces, pairs, dozens or packs) of that product. Some customs duties are a combination of *ad valorem* and specific duties and are called *compound* or *mixed customs duties*.

> For example, Industria applies a duty of €1 per kilogram of imported chocolate and a duty of €30 on each imported smartphone. Both of these are specific customs duties.

The customs duties or tariffs imposed by a WTO Member that are due on importation are set out in that Member's national 'tariff' or 'customs tariff'. A customs tariff is a structured list of product descriptions and their corresponding custom duties.

Many WTO Members have an online database of the customs duties they apply, for example the TARIC database of the European Union. The website of the World Customs Organization (WCO) gives easy access to many of these databases.

3.2.1 Tariff negotiations

WTO law and, in particular, the GATT 1994, does not prohibit the imposition of customs duties. Customs duties, unlike quantitative restrictions, represent an instrument of protection against imports that is generally allowed under the GATT 1994. Article XXVIII *bis* of the GATT 1994 does, however, call upon WTO Members to negotiate the reduction of customs duties to increase market access for products. The eight rounds of trade negotiations under the GATT 1947 were very successful in reducing the average customs duties of developed countries on industrial products from 22 per cent to less than 4 per cent *ad valorem*. Nevertheless, customs duties remain an important barrier to international trade for several reasons, *inter alia* because (1) many developing countries still maintain relatively high tariffs, (2) high tariffs remain on certain sensitive products (known as *tariff peaks*), and (3) tariffs tend to increase with the level of processing that products have undergone (known as *tariff escalation*). Thus, further negotiations on the reduction on tariffs are necessary. The basic rules governing tariff negotiations are:

51

- the MFN treatment obligation of Article I of the GATT 1994 (see Section 2.2); and
- the principle of reciprocity and mutual advantage.

Note, however, that in tariff negotiations between developed and developing country Members, the principle of relative reciprocity applies: developing-country Members are expected to 'reciprocate' only to the extent consistent with their development, financial and trade needs. The first tariff negotiations in the context of the GATT 1947 were conducted on a request-and-offer basis regarding selected goods. Later tariff negotiations focused on reaching agreement on a formula to lower customs duties across the board.

In the context of the ongoing Doha Round negotiations, WTO Members are, for example with regard to the lowering of customs duties on non-agricultural products, trying to agree on the so-called *Swiss formula*, which would require larger cuts of higher customs duties than of lower customs duties.

3.2.2 Tariff concessions

The results of successful tariff negotiations are referred to as 'tariff concessions' or 'tariff bindings'. A tariff concession, or a tariff binding, is a commitment not to raise the customs duty on a certain product above an agreed level. The tariff concessions or bindings of a Member are set out in that Member's Schedule of Concessions, also known as its Goods Schedule. Most Schedules are structured according to the Harmonized Commodity Description and Coding System (known as the 'Harmonized System' or 'HS'), discussed in Section 3.2.3.1.

The Schedules of Concessions resulting from the Uruguay Round negotiations are all annexed to the Marrakesh Protocol to the GATT 1994 and are an integral part of the GATT 1994.

> As stated by the Appellate Body in *EC – Computer Equipment (1998)*, 'the fact that Members' Schedules are an integral part of the GATT 1994 indicates that, while each Schedule represents the tariff commitments made by *one* Member, they represent a common agreement among *all* Members'.

Therefore, Members' Goods Schedules are interpreted in accordance with customary international law rules on treaty interpretation, codified in Articles 31 and 32 of the Vienna Convention on the Law of Treaties, in order to ascertain the common intentions of the Members (see Section 8.2). Members' Schedules of Concessions can be consulted on the WTO website.

Article II:1(a) of the GATT 1994 provides that Members must accord to products imported from other Members treatment no less favourable than that provided for in their Goods Schedule. Article II:1(b), first sentence, of the GATT 1994, provides that products described in Part I of the Schedule of any Member shall, on importation, be exempt from ordinary customs duties in excess of those set out in the

Schedule. This means that products may not be subjected to customs duties above the tariff concessions or bindings.

The objective of both provisions is to protect the commitments on the reduction of customs duties that have been made during the tariff negotiations and to provide certainty as to the maximum customs duties that a WTO Member can impose on a product. Naturally, WTO Members may impose customs duties that are lower than their tariff concessions. In fact, many customs duties actually applied by Members are lower than the tariff concessions they agreed on. Finally, note that tariff concessions can be amended or withdrawn. The applicable requirements and procedure are set out in Article XXVIII of the GATT 1994.

> The Schedule of Concessions of Industria provides that its tariff binding for cocoa powder is 8 per cent *ad valorem*. That means that the currently applied customs duty of 6 per cent *ad valorem* (as set out in Industria's national customs tariff) is consistent with its obligations under Article II:1(a) and Article II:1(b), first sentence, of the GATT 1994. Industria is free to raise its applied customs duty up to, but no higher than, 8 per cent *ad valorem* without violating its obligations under these provisions.

3.2.3 *Imposition of custom duties*

In addition to the rules to protect tariff concessions, WTO law also provides for rules on the manner in which customs duties must be imposed. The imposition of customs duties may require three determinations to be made:

- the determination of the proper classification of the imported good;
- the determination of the customs value of the imported good; and
- the determination of the origin of the imported good.

3.2.3.1 Customs classification

Because customs duties may differ from product to product, the correct imposition of customs duties requires the determination of the proper customs classification of the imported product. WTO law does not *specifically* address the issue of customs classification. However, in classifying products for customs purposes, Members have, of course, to comply with their general obligations under WTO law, such as the MFN treatment obligation (see Section 2.2).

Specific rules on customs classification can be found in the WCO's International Convention on the Harmonized Commodity Description and Coding System (the 'Harmonized System' or 'HS') signed in Brussels in 1983 and most recently amended in 2012. Almost all WTO Members are a party to this international convention and therefore follow the same rules for customs classification. Although the Harmonized System is not a WTO agreement, the Appellate Body held in *EC – Chicken Cuts (2005)* and confirmed in *China – Auto Parts (2009)* that it is relevant for the interpretation of Goods Schedules and the tariff bindings contained therein.

In *EC – Chicken Cuts (2005)*, the proper customs classification of frozen boneless chicken cuts impregnated
with salt was at issue. The European Communities had
classified this product under the tariff heading 02.07
'Meat and edible offal, of poultry of heading No. 0105,
fresh, chilled or frozen', whereas the complainants
alleged that the appropriate tariff heading was 02.10
'Meat and edible meat offal, salted, in brine, dried,
smoked; edible flours and meals of meat or meat offal'.
Under the latter tariff heading, the applicable customs
duty was lower than under the heading that applied
according to the European Communities. The latter
argued that the key element under heading 02.10 was
preservation and therefore the term 'salted' implied that
the meat should be impregnated with salt sufficient to
ensure long-term preservation. The complainants contested this interpretation and, after examining the
Harmonized System, both the panel and the Appellate
Body agreed with them. Therefore, the frozen boneless
chicken cuts impregnated with salt were held to fall
under tariff heading 02.10, to which the lower customs
duty applied.

3.2.3.2 Customs valuation

Because customs duties are often *ad valorem*, the value of
imported products must be determined in order to be able to
calculate the customs duties due. WTO law does provide for
rules on customs valuation. These are set out in Article VII of

the GATT 1994, entitled 'Valuation for Customs Purposes', and in the Agreement on the Implementation of Article VII of the GATT 1994 (commonly known as the Customs Valuation Agreement).

The primary basis for the determination of the customs value of imported goods, as set out in Article 1 of the Customs Valuation Agreement, is the 'transaction value' of these goods; that is, the price actually paid or payable for the goods when sold for export to the importing country. This price is normally shown in the invoice, contract or purchase order. Articles 2–7 of the Customs Valuation Agreement provide alternative methods for determining the customs value whenever it cannot be established on the basis of the transaction value. However, certain bases for determining the customs value of a product are explicitly prohibited under Article 7.2(a)–(g), namely: the selling price in the country of importation of the product produced in that country, the price of the product on the domestic market of the country of exportation, minimum customs values, or arbitrary or fictitious values.

3.2.3.3 Rules of origin

The determination of the origin of an imported product can be important because the applicable customs duties may vary according to the country of origin of the product. For example, products originating in developing countries commonly benefit from lower customs duties or even duty-free importation under the Generalized System of Preferences (see Section 4.8). Similarly, no customs duties apply to goods from Members that are part of the same free-trade area or customs union. Aside from its use for the application of preferential customs duties, the determination of origin is also necessary for non-preferential trade policy instruments, such as antidumping duties, countervailing duties and safeguard measures. However, the determination of the origin of a product is often not an easy task.

Is a smartphone, of which the case, screen and electronics were made in Industria, which is subsequently assembled in Agricola and to which the software is added in Alpinia, of Industrian, Agricolan or Alpinian origin?

With respect to *non-preferential* rules of origin, the WTO Agreement on Rules of Origin provides for an ambitious but as-yet not completed work programme for the harmonization of these rules meant to facilitate the determination of the country of origin of a product. In the interim, Article 2 of this Agreement contains an extensive set of disciplines on the application and administration of non-preferential rules of origin; for example, non-discrimination, transparency, non-retroactivity and reasonable and impartial administration. After harmonized non-preferential rules of origin have been agreed upon, these disciplines will continue to apply. With regard to *preferential* rules of origin, Annex II to the Agreement on Rules of Origin contains a more limited set of disciplines. Preferential rules of origin are not covered by the harmonization work programme.

National rules of origin, which the WTO seeks to harmonize, now often determine the origin of a product based on the country where the product is either wholly or predominantly obtained or where it has undergone its last substantial transformation. Members may regard a change in tariff classification, a particular technical, manufacturing or processing operation, and/or a specific percentage of value added as indicating where the last substantial transformation occurred.

3.2.4 Other duties and charges

In addition to ordinary customs duties, imported products are sometimes subject to 'other duties and charges'. Other duties and charges refer to financial charges or taxes on imported products other than ordinary customs duties, for example, import surcharges, security deposits, customs fees, foreign exchange fees and statistical taxes. According to Article II:1(b), second sentence, of the GATT 1994, *no* other duties or charges may be imposed *in excess of* those (1) already imposed at the 'date of this Agreement' (15 April 1994 or the date of accession to the WTO) or (2) provided for in mandatory legislation in force on that date. To ensure transparency regarding the nature and level of such 'other duties and charges', the Understanding on the Interpretation of Article II:1(b) of the GATT 1994 requires Members to record in their Goods Schedules all 'other duties and charges' imposed on products subject to a tariff binding at the levels applying on 15 April 1994 or on the date of accession to the WTO. Other duties and charges not so recorded, or in excess of the recorded levels, are prohibited.

There are, however, a number of exceptions to the rule that Members may not impose 'other duties or charges' not properly recorded in their Good Schedules or in excess of recorded levels. In accordance with Article II:2 of the GATT 1994, Members may – in spite of their obligations under Article II:1(b), second sentence – impose on imported products:

- any financial charge that is not in excess of the internal tax imposed on the like domestic product (known as *border tax adjustment*);
- WTO consistent anti-dumping or countervailing duties; or
- fees or other charges 'commensurate' with (i.e. matching) the cost of the services supplied.

With regard to the latter fees or other charges, Article VIII:1(a) of the GATT 1994 as well as Article 6.2 of the Agreement on Trade Facilitation also provide that these fees or other charges shall be limited in amount to the (approximate) cost of the services rendered.

3.3 Export duties and charges

Although much less common than customs duties and other duties and charges on imports, WTO Members sometimes impose customs duties or other charges on exports (known in brief as *export duties*). Export duties are financial charges on products due because of their exportation. The imposition of export duties fell largely into disuse in the mid-nineteenth century but has increased in recent years, particularly in respect of agricultural products and raw materials that are in short supply on the world market.

Note that there are no WTO rules prohibiting or specifically regulating export duties. However, general

GATT obligations, such as MFN treatment, apply also to export duties (see Section 2.2). In addition, some WTO Members, including China and Russia, have taken on additional obligations in their Accession Protocols in this regard.

The issue whether export duties imposed by China were inconsistent with the additional obligation China took on in its Accession Protocol, arose in *China – Raw Materials (2012)* and again in *China – Rare Earths (2014)*. These disputes concerned, respectively, export duties on certain raw materials (bauxite, coke, fluorspar, magnesium, manganese, silicon metal, zinc and yellow phosphorus) and export duties on various forms of rare earths, tungsten and molybdenum. These materials are used *inter alia* in devices such as computer memory chips, mobile phones and rechargeable batteries, and global demand for them has grown exponentially in the past twenty years. The panels in both cases found that the China's export duties were inconsistent with the additional obligations China had undertaken in its Accession Protocol.

3.4 Quantitative restrictions on trade in goods

A quantitative restriction is a measure that limits the quantity of a product that may be imported or exported. A quantitative restriction can take the form of a quota but may also be a general import or export prohibition or another restriction on importation or exportation. Unlike customs duties, which are not prohibited (see Section 3.2.1), Article XI:1 of the GATT 1994 sets out a general prohibition on quantitative restrictions, whether on imports or exports.

An Industrian regulation that limits the amount of imported smartphones to 1 million per year and an Agricolan law that prohibits the importation of chocolate bars are both quantitative restrictions within the meaning of Article XI of the GATT 1994 and are therefore in principle prohibited.

The prohibition of Article XI:1 of the GATT 1994 is broad. According to firmly established case law, quantitative restrictions that do not *actually* impede trade (e.g. because the level of imports or exports allowed is higher than the current level of trade), as well as quantitative restrictions of a de facto nature, are prohibited under Article XI:1 of the GATT 1994. De facto quantitative restrictions are those that are not in the form of blanket prohibitions or precise numerical limits but nevertheless have a *limiting effect* on importation or exportation. However, not every measure placing a burden on importation or exportation is inconsistent with Article XI; only measures that *limit the quantity* of a product being imported or exported are. This limitation need not be demonstrated by quantifying the effects of the measure at issue but can be demonstrated through the design, architecture and revealing structure of the measure. Note, however, that restrictions in the form of duties, taxes or other charges are explicitly not covered by the prohibition of Article XI:1 of the GATT 1994.

In *China – Raw Materials (2012)*, the panel found that the minimum export price requirement imposed by China on exporters of bauxite, coke, fluorspar, magnesium, silicon carbide, yellow phosphorus and zinc was a quantitative restriction on exports, in violation of Article XI:1 of the GATT 1994.

Note that a *tariff quota* (that is, a quantity that can be imported at a specific customs duty) is not a quantitative restriction and is therefore not prohibited under Article XI of the GATT 1994. Tariff quotas are not quantitative restrictions despite the fact that they may negatively affect the conditions for importation. This is so because they take the form of varying *customs duties* on specific quantities of imports. Recall that Article XI excludes 'customs duties, taxes or other charges' from its scope.

An Industrian regulation that provides that 500 000 smartphones may be imported per year at a customs duty of 7 per cent *ad valorem* and that, on all imported smartphones exceeding this limit, a customs duty of 15 per cent is due, sets a tariff quota. Such a quota is not prohibited under Article XI:1.

Note, however, that the rules of Article XIII of the GATT 1994 on the non-discriminatory administration of quantitative restrictions, which are discussed in Section 3.4.1, are applicable also to tariff quotas.

3.4.1 *Non-discriminatory administration*

Although quantitative restrictions are, as a general rule, prohibited, there are many exceptions to this prohibition. This explains why Article XIII of the GATT 1994 sets out rules on the administration of quantitative restrictions (and tariff quotas). Article XIII:1 of the GATT 1994 provides that quantitative restrictions, when applied, must be administered in a non-discriminatory manner. Article XIII:1 requires that if a Member imposes a quantitative restriction on products to or from another Member, 'like products' to or from all other countries must be 'similarly prohibited or restricted'. According to the chapeau of Article XIII:2 of the GATT 1994, the distribution of trade still allowed should be as close as possible to what would have been the distribution of trade in the absence of the quantitative restriction (or tariff quota).

Furthermore, Article XIII:2 sets out a number of requirements to be met when imposing quotas (or tariff quotas) on imports. Article XIII:2(d) provides that, if no agreement can be reached with all Members having a substantial interest in supplying the product concerned, the quota (or tariff quota) must be allocated among these Members on the basis of their share of the trade in that product during a previous representative period. According to the case law, quota shares can also be allocated to Members that do not have a substantial interest in supplying the product. When doing so, a Member must comply with the requirements of Article XIII:1 and the chapeau of Article XIII:2, discussed earlier.

> This year, Agricola has decided to impose an import quota on smartphones of 800 000 units per year. In the previous three years, Industria and Alpinia had shares of 40 per cent and 60 per cent, respectively, of Agricola's imports of smartphones. In the absence of agreement with Industria and Alpinia on the allocation of the quota, Agricola must allocate a share of the quota of 320 000 units to Industria and of 480 000 units to Alpinia.

3.4.2 Import licensing procedures

Quotas (and tariff quotas) are usually administered through import licensing procedures. A trader who wishes to import a product that is subject to a quota (or tariff quota) must usually apply for an import license (that is, a permit to import). The Agreement on Import Licensing Procedures, commonly known as the Import Licensing Agreement, sets out, in Article 1 thereof, general rules for the application and administration of import licensing procedures, including the requirement in Article 1.3 that rules for import licensing procedures be neutral in application and administered in a fair and equitable manner. The Import Licensing Agreement distinguishes between automatic and non-automatic import licensing procedures. *Automatic import licensing* is import licensing in which approval of the application is granted *in all cases*, whereas, in the case of *non-automatic import licensing*, approval is subject to certain conditions and is thus *not* always granted. Import licensing procedures for quotas (and tariff quotas) are by definition non-automatic import licensing procedures since approval for importation is only granted to the extent that the quota is not yet full. Articles 2 and 3 of the Import Licensing Agreement set out specific rules that apply to automatic and non-automatic import licensing procedures, respectively.

3.5 Other non-tariff barriers to trade in goods

In addition to customs duties and other duties and charges and quantitative restrictions, market access is also hindered by 'other non-tariff barriers' to trade in goods, including:

- technical barriers to trade in goods and sanitary and phytosanitary measures;
- lack of transparency in national regulation;
- unfair and arbitrary application of national trade laws and regulations;
- customs formalities and procedures;
- government procurement rules and practices; and
- other measures or actions.

The rules concerning technical barriers to trade, as well as sanitary and phytosanitary measures are discussed in Sections 6.2. and 6.3.

3.5.1 Lack of transparency

Ignorance, uncertainty or confusion with respect to the trade laws, regulations and procedures applicable in actual or potential export markets is an important barrier to trade in goods. To ensure a high level of transparency of its Members' trade laws, regulations and procedures, most WTO agreements provide for rules that require Members to:

- continually inform the WTO Secretariat of new rules or modifications of existing rules (notification requirement);
- publish their trade rules promptly and before applying them (publication requirement); and
- provide for enquiry points where other Members and their traders can acquire information on the relevant laws and regulations affecting trade.

Some WTO Agreements, such as the TBT Agreement and the SPS Agreement contain additional transparency obligations. For example, measures covered by those Agreements must be notified to the WTO Secretariat before they are adopted, to give other WTO Members the opportunity to express any comments or objections in time.

Finally, the transparency of Members' trade policies, laws and procedures is also significantly improved by the periodic trade policy reviews of each Member under the Trade Policy Review Mechanism (see Section 7.3.4).

3.5.2 Unfair and arbitrary application of national trade laws and regulations

It is clear that the unfair and arbitrary application of national trade measures and the degree of uncertainty and unpredictability this generates for other Members and their traders also constitutes a significant barrier to market access. Therefore, Article X:3 of the GATT 1994 provides for:

- a requirement of uniform, impartial and reasonable administration of national trade rules; and
- a requirement of procedures for the objective and impartial review and possible correction of the administration of national customs rules by judicial, arbitral or administrative tribunals.

> For example, the panel in *Dominican Republic – Import and Sale of Cigarettes (2005)* found the requirement of 'reasonable administration' to be violated due to the fact that the Dominican Republic authorities did not support their decisions regarding the determination of the tax base for imported cigarettes by resorting to the domestic law in force at the time and that they decided to disregard retail selling prices of imported cigarettes. This was found to be not 'in accordance with reason'.

3.5.3 *Customs formalities and procedures*

Customs formalities and procedures can constitute formidable barriers to market access. The losses that traders suffer through delays at borders and complicated or unnecessary documentation requirements and other customs procedures and formalities are estimated to exceed in many cases the costs of tariffs. However, WTO law currently contains few rules on customs formalities and procedures aimed at mitigating their adverse impact on trade. A very general obligation in Article VIII:2 of the GATT 1994 requires Members to review the operation of their laws and regulations in light of the acknowledged need for (1) minimizing the incidence and complexity of customs formalities and (2) decreasing and simplifying documentation requirements. Article VIII:3 of the GATT 1994 furthermore requires penalties for breaches of customs regulations and procedural requirements to be *proportional* to the severity of the breach.

Negotiations, in the context of the Doha Round, to establish specific rules to simplify customs formalities and procedures resulted, at the Bali Ministerial Conference in December 2013, in the Agreement on Trade Facilitation. In November 2014, the WTO Members adopted a Protocol of Amendment to insert this new Agreement into Annex 1A of the WTO Agreement. The Agreement on Trade Facilitation will enter into force once two-thirds of Members have completed their domestic ratification process. This Agreement aims to facilitate the movement, release and clearance of goods, including goods in transit, and promote customs cooperation. It also contains provisions for technical assistance and capacity-building in this area for developing-country Members. It has been estimated that by removing barriers to trade and cutting red tape at the borders, the Trade Facilitation Agreement could stimulate the world economy by more than US$1 trillion and create 21 million jobs.

3.5.4 Government procurement rules and practices

The national laws and practices according to which a government procures goods for its own use are often significant barriers to trade. Governments frequently use their procurement activities to stimulate the national economy or promote employment by purchasing domestic rather than imported goods. Because Article III:8(a) of the GATT 1994 exempts government procurement from the national treatment obligation (see Section 2.4), this important area of economic activity, representing 10–15 per cent of gross domestic product (GDP) on average, can be subject to discriminatory laws, procedures and practices.

To address this gap in the multilateral disciplines, a number of WTO Members have negotiated a plurilateral Agreement on Government Procurement, which contains, *inter alia*, obligations of non-discrimination and transparency in government procurement activities in respect of both goods and services. This agreement is binding only on those forty-five WTO Members that are parties to this agreement.

Each party to the Agreement on Government Procurement has a Coverage Schedule defining the scope of its commitments under this agreement. These Schedules set out for each party:

- the procuring entities covered by the Agreement;
- the goods, services and construction services covered by the Agreement;
- the threshold values above which procurement activities are covered by the Agreement; and
- exceptions to the coverage.

These Coverage Schedules are an integral part of the Agreement on Government Procurement and available on the WTO website.

In April 2014, a revision to the Agreement on Government Procurement came into force, extending its scope of application to more entities and lower contract values. The resulting gains in market access are estimated at between US$80 and 100 billion per year.

3.5.5 *Other measures or actions*

Aside from the above-mentioned measures, the category of 'other non-tariff barriers' to market access also includes many other measures or actions/omissions. Examples of 'other non-tariff barriers' are (1) preshipment inspection, (2) marks of origin, (3) measures relating to transit shipments, (4) operations of State trading enterprises, (5) trade-related investment measures, and (6) exchange controls or exchange restrictions. WTO law contains a number of rules addressing such 'other non-tariff barriers' in order to minimize their trade restrictive effect.

3.6 Market access barriers to trade in services

As is the case with trade in goods, trade in services is often subject to restrictions. Unlike trade in goods, however, trade-restrictive measures applied at the border are barely significant for trade in services. Instead, barriers to trade in services primarily result from the vast range of domestic regulations that govern the production and consumption of services. WTO law and the GATS in particular, provide rules and disciplines on barriers to trade in services. A distinction must be made between *market access barriers* and *other barriers to trade* in services.

Note that most internal regulation of services does not constitute a GATS-inconsistent barrier to trade in services. As will be seen later, the market access obligations of the GATS are much less far-reaching than those of the GATT. This may be explained by the fact that regulation of many service sectors touches on important areas of public policy, such as consumer protection and public health and safety. In fact, the Preamble to the GATS explicitly recognizes the *right* of WTO Members to regulate services in their territories to meet national public policy objectives.

The rules on market access barriers to trade in services are laid down in Article XVI of the GATS. Note that *not all* barriers to market access are 'market access barriers' within the meaning of Article XVI. Instead, Article XVI:2 of the GATS contains an exhaustive list of 'market access barriers' in subparagraphs (a) to (f). This list includes:

- five types of quantitative restrictions, namely, limitations on the number of service suppliers that may be active in a specific market; limitations on the total value of service transactions; limitations on the total number of service operations; limitations on the number of natural persons that may be employed by a service supplier or in a service sector; and limitations on the participation of foreign capital in enterprises supplying services; and
- one type of restriction that limits the supply of services to specific forms of legal entity or joint venture.

In *US – Gambling (2005)*, the panel found that, by maintaining measures that *prohibited* the supply of online gambling services, the United States effectively limited to zero the number of service suppliers and service operations relating to that service. On appeal, the Appellate Body agreed that a measure equivalent to a zero quota is a market access barrier within the meaning of Article XVI:2.

Market access barriers sometimes specifically restrict market access for foreign services and service suppliers. However, often market access barriers restrict access for both foreign and domestic services and service suppliers. Such non-discriminatory measures are also covered by the concept of 'market access barriers' under Article XVI. The quantitative restrictions covered by Article XVI:2 may be expressed numerically or in the other forms specified in this provision, for example, through certain economic criteria that must be met to gain market access ('economic needs test'). However, measures that impede market access by imposing requirements relating to the quality of services or the qualifications of service suppliers are not market access barriers within the meaning of Article XVI.

An Agricolan regulation that limits the number of foreign coffeehouses in its cities to ten per every 1 million inhabitants, as well as a regulation that limits the number of coffeehouses (whether foreign or domestic) to fifty for every 1 million inhabitants, are market access barriers within the meaning of Article XVI of the GATS.

> By contrast, a law requiring that the serving staff of all coffeehouses in Agricola be fluent in the Agricolan language and be trained in the traditional method of brewing coffee is not a market access barrier within the meaning of Article XVI of the GATS.

It is important to note that the GATS does not provide for a general prohibition on the market access barriers listed in Article XVI:2. Whether a Member may maintain or adopt a market access barrier with regard to a specific service depends on whether, and if so to what extent, that Member has made market access commitments with regard to the service sector concerned. These commitments are set out in a Member's Services Schedule (see Section 2.5). When a Member makes a market access commitment, it binds the level of market access specified in its Services Schedule (see Article XVI:1 of the GATS) and agrees not to impose any market access barrier listed in Article XVI:2 that would restrict access to the market beyond the level specified in the relevant commitment. Market access commitments are often accompanied by limitations (either generally, recorded in the 'Horizontal Commitments' part of the Services Schedule, or for specific services and modes of supply, recorded in the sector-specific part of the Services Schedule). It is therefore possible that some market access barriers are permitted despite the fact that a market access commitment has been made in the relevant service sector. In assessing the scope of the market access commitments made, it is important to look both at the sector-specific part and the 'Horizontal Commitments' part of a Member's Services Schedule. If a WTO Member has not made any market access commitment in a specific service sector, then there is no prohibition on market access barriers in the sector concerned.

Table 3.1 *Excerpt of the Services Schedule of Industria*

I HORIZONTAL COMMITMENTS

Sector or subsector	Limitations on market access	Limitations on national treatment
All sectors included in this Schedule	(4) Unbound, except for specialists, being natural persons with essential technical or professional skills assessed in terms of the applicant's employment experience and qualifications, and the scarcity of such skills in Industria.	(3) Eligibility for subsidies may be limited to legal persons established within the national territory.

II SECTOR-SPECIFIC COMMITMENTS

Sector or subsector	Limitations on market access	Limitations on national treatment
Human health services (UN CPC 931) ...		
93122 Specialized medical services	(1) None (2) None (3) Subject to a maximum of thirty foreign hospitals (4) Unbound, except as indicated in the horizontal section	(1) Three years of professional practice in Industria required (2) None (3) Industrian nationality required to establish an independent practice (4) Unbound

(1) cross-border, (2) consumption abroad, (3) commercial presence, (4) natural persons

Examine the excerpt of Industria's Services Schedule provided here. In light of this Schedule, Article XVI of the GATS would prohibit Industria to limit the value of specialist psychiatric services provided to Industrian patients via the Internet to 1 million Industrian dollars per year. Article XVI would also prohibit Industria to refuse to allow the establishment of a foreign cardiac hospital as long as there were still less than thirty foreign hospitals or other entities providing specialized medical services established in its territory. Industria could, however, refuse to allow the establishment of the thirty-first such hospital or entity. Industria would also be free to restrict the entry of oncologists wishing to provide consultancy medical services to hospitals in its territory if there was no scarcity of qualified and experienced oncologists in Industria. Finally, a regulation requiring a minimum number of obstetricians and pediatricians to staff maternity hospitals in its territory, or setting specific qualification requirements for such specialists, would not be caught by the market access obligation of Article XVI because these measures are not 'market access barriers' within the meaning of Article XVI:2 of the GATS.

Current market access commitments for trade in services, such as those negotiated in the context of the Uruguay Round, are not very far-reaching. Most WTO Members have only committed themselves to maintaining the existing level of market access. It is therefore not surprising that Article XIX of the GATS calls on Members to engage in negotiations aiming at the progressive liberalization of trade in services. Negotiations on the liberalization of services follow a request-and-offer approach. It is accepted that developing-country Members undertake fewer and more limited market access commitments than developed-country Members. Currently, negotiations on further liberalization of trade in services are part of the Doha Round. The results of services negotiations are, as indicated earlier, set out in Members' Services Schedules.

> For example, in the second column of the sector-specific part of its Services Schedule, Industria has recorded a limitation to market access for specialized medical services for the third mode of service supply (i.e. commercial presence) by restricting to thirty the number of foreign suppliers of specialist medical services that may establish themselves in its territory. It has also recorded that the fourth mode of service supply (presence of natural persons) is 'unbound, except as indicated in the horizontal section'; that is, no specific commitments are made for this mode, aside from the general commitments set out in the horizontal section of Industria's Services Schedule. In the horizontal section of its Services Schedule, Industria has indicated that the fourth mode of service supply is 'unbound' except for qualified and experienced specialists whose skills are scarce in Industria.

The Services Schedule of each Member is annexed to the GATS and forms an integral part thereof. These Schedules are therefore to be interpreted according to the customary international rules on treaty interpretation, codified in Articles 31 and 32 of the Vienna Convention on the Law of Treaties.

In *US – Gambling (2005)*, the United States emphasized that it had not intended to schedule a commitment for gambling services when it inscribed the sector 'recreational services, except sporting' in its Services Schedule. Although the panel had sympathy for this, it pointed out that scheduled commitments are reciprocal and result from mutually advantageous negotiations. Thus, the scope of a specific commitment cannot depend on what a Member intended or did not intend to do at the time of the negotiations, but instead depends on the *common* intent of all negotiating parties. This common intent is determined according to the rules of interpretation set out in Articles 31 and 32 of the Vienna Convention on the Law of Treaties. The Appellate Body agreed with this approach.

All Members' Services Schedules can be found on the WTO website.

Like tariff concessions for goods, market access commitments for services can also be modified or withdrawn. To do so, the procedure set out in Article XXI of the GATS must be followed.

3.7 Other barriers to trade in services

In addition to market access barriers within the meaning of Article XVI of the GATS, trade in services can also be impeded directly or indirectly by a wide array of other barriers. With regard to a number of these other barriers, WTO law, and in particular, the GATS, provides for specific rules. Some of these rules have general application; they apply in all services sectors, including those in which no specific commitments have been undertaken. For example, Article III of the GATS contains a general transparency obligation which requires the prompt publication of all measures of general application affecting trade in services and obliges Members to establish enquiry points to provide information on laws and regulations affecting trade in services. Furthermore, Article VI:2(a) of the GATS requires Members to maintain objective and impartial procedures, whether judicial or administrative, which allow service suppliers to challenge administrative decisions affecting them. Other GATS rules on 'other barriers to trade in services' apply only if and to the extent that the WTO Member concerned has made market access or national treatment commitments. For example, Article VI:1 of the GATS requires Members to ensure that all measures of general application affecting trade in services with regard to which specific commitments were made are administered in a *reasonable, objective and impartial* manner. These GATS rules strongly resemble the GATT rules set out in Section 3.5.2.

Furthermore, as noted earlier, trade in services is primarily restricted by internal regulation. Most internal

79

regulations do not constitute market access barriers within the meaning of Article XVI:2 of the GATS. Apart from the rules concerning transparency and the rules on unfair and arbitrary application, the GATS currently only provides for a few other rules applicable to internal regulations which do not constitute market access barriers. The most important of these disciplines is contained in Article VI:5 of the GATS, which concerns licensing requirements, qualification requirements and technical standards that affect specific commitments undertaken by a Member. These requirements and standards must:

- be based on objective and transparent criteria, such as competence and the ability to supply the service;
- not be more burdensome than necessary to ensure the quality of the service; and
- in the case of licensing procedures, not be, in themselves, a restriction on the supply of the service.

Article VI:4 of the GATS gives the Council for Trade in Services a broad and ambitious mandate to develop the multilateral disciplines necessary to ensure that licensing requirements, qualification requirements and procedures and technical standards do not constitute *unnecessary barriers* to trade in services. Such disciplines have thus far only been developed in the accountancy sector.

Note that Article VII of the GATS encourages and facilitates the recognition of diplomas and professional certificates of foreign service suppliers.

Finally, recall that the plurilateral Agreement on Government Procurement covers the government procurement activities of its parties in the services sectors listed in their Coverage Schedules (see Section 3.5.4).

Further reading

Bartels, L., and Häberli, C. (2010) 'Binding tariff preferences for developing countries under Article II GATT', *Journal of International Economic Law* 13(4) 969–995.

Matsushita, M. (2011) 'Export controls of natural resources and the WTO/GATT disciplines', *Asian Journal of WTO and International Health Law and Policy* 6 281–312.

Matsushita, M. (2012) 'A note on the Appellate Body report in the Chinese Minerals Export Restrictions case', *Trade Law and Development* 4(2) 400–420.

Pauwelyn, P. (2005) 'Rien ne Va Plus? Distinguishing domestic regulation from market access in GATT and GATS', *World Trade Review* 4(2) 131–170.

Regan, H. D. (2007) 'A gambling paradox: why an origin-neutral "zero-quota"' is not a quota under GATS Article XVI', *Journal of World Trade* 41(6) 1297–1317.

Roessler, F. (2010) 'India – Additional and Extra-Additional Duties on Imports from the United States', *World Trade Review* 9 265–272.

Rovetta, D. (2009) 'Some reflections on customs classification and the Harmonized System as tools for interpreting the Schedules of Commitments under GATT Article II', *Legal Issues of Economic Integration* 36(1) 7–22.

Rovetta, D., Sud, J., and Vermulst, E. (2009) 'WTO dispute settlement with respect to customs matters', *Global Trade and Customs Journal* 4(4) 99–111.

Van Damme, I. (2007) 'The interpretation of Schedules of Commitments', *Journal of World Trade* 41(1) 1–52.

Vranes, E. (2009) 'The WTO and regulatory freedom: WTO disciplines on market access, non-discrimination and domestic regulation relating to trade in goods and services', *Journal of International Economic Law* 12(4) 953–987.

Chapter 4

Trade liberalization and other societal values and interests

4.1 Introduction

Trade liberalization often facilitates the promotion and protection of other important societal values and interests, such as public health, consumer safety, the environment, employment, economic development and national security. More trade often means that more, cheaper, better, healthier, safer and/or environmentally friendlier products and services will be available on the domestic market. More trade also means more economic activity and development and generates the resources that enable governments effectively to promote and protect societal values and interests.

Trade liberalization, with its principles of non-discrimination and rules on market access, however, also regularly clashes with the aforementioned other societal values and interests. Governments frequently adopt legislation or take measures that restrict trade in goods and/or services in order to protect, for example, public health, public morals, employment or national security.

WTO law provides rules to reconcile trade liberalization with other important societal values and interests. These rules take the form of wide-ranging exceptions to, *inter alia*, the basic WTO disciplines discussed in Chapters 2 and 3 (the non-discrimination obligations and the market access rules). There are five main categories of exceptions:

- the 'general exceptions' of Article XX of the GATT 1994 and Article XIV of the GATS;
- the exceptions for national and international security of Article XXI of the GATT 1994 and Article XIV *bis* of the GATS;
- the exceptions for safeguard measures of Article XIX of the GATT 1994 and the Agreement on Safeguards;
- the exceptions for balance of payments measures of Articles XII and XVIII:B of the GATT 1994 and Article XII of the GATS;
- the exceptions for regional trade agreements of Article XXIV of the GATT 1994 and Article V of the GATS; and
- the exceptions for economic development set out in 'special and differential treatment' provisions and the 'Enabling Clause'.

These exceptions differ in scope and nature. Some allow deviation from all GATT or GATS obligations; others allow deviation from specific obligations only; some are of indefinite duration; others are temporary. However, all these exceptions have in common that they allow WTO Members, under specific conditions, to adopt and maintain measures that protect other important societal values and interests, even though these measures conflict with substantive disciplines imposed by the GATT 1994 or the GATS. These exceptions thus clearly allow Members, under specific conditions, to give priority to certain societal values and interests over trade liberalization. These exceptions will be discussed further in the following sections.

4.2 General exceptions under Article XX of the GATT 1994

The most important exceptions from GATT obligations 'reconciling' trade liberalization with other societal values and interests are the 'general exceptions' of Article XX of the GATT 1994. Article XX of the GATT 1994 allows, under specific conditions, deviation from *any* GATT obligation be it Article I:1 (MFN treatment), Article II:1 (tariff concessions), Articles III:2 and III:4 (national treatment), Article XI:1 (quantitative restrictions) or any other obligation under the GATT 1994. Article XX of the GATT 1994 is not available to justify inconsistencies with any other WTO agreement unless it has been expressly or implicitly incorporated into such agreement. The Agreement on Trade Related Investment Measures is the only other WTO Agreement which expressly incorporates Article XX of the GATT 1994. Article XX can thus be invoked to justify inconsistencies with this Agreement. As the Appellate Body ruled in *China – Publications and Audiovisual Products (2010)*, certain provisions of the China Accession Protocol implicitly incorporate Article XX, and the latter can therefore be invoked by China to justify a breach of the obligations under these provisions. As the Appellate Body made clear in *China – Raw Materials (2012)* and *China – Rare Earths (2014)*, other provisions of the China Accession Protocol cannot be read to incorporate Article XX of the GATT 1994.

As noted by the panel in *US – Section 337 Tariff Act (1989)*, Article XX provides for *limited and conditional*

> *exceptions* from obligations under other GATT provisions. The exceptions are 'limited' because the list of justification grounds in Article XX is exhaustive. The exceptions are 'conditional' in that Article XX only provides for justification of an otherwise GATT-inconsistent measure when the conditions set out in Article XX are met.

In determining whether a measure that is otherwise GATT-inconsistent can be justified under Article XX of the GATT 1994, one must always examine:

- first, whether this measure can provisionally be justified under one of the specific justification grounds listed in paragraphs (a) to (j) of Article XX; and, if so,
- second, whether the application of this measure meets the requirements of the 'chapeau' (i.e. the introductory clause) of Article XX.

Article XX of the GATT is in essence a *balancing* provision. According to well-established case law, central to the interpretation of Article XX is the balance to be realized between trade liberalization on the one hand and other societal values and interests on the other. This means that a (too) narrow interpretation of this exception is as inappropriate as a (too) broad interpretation.

Article XX of the GATT 1994 sets out, in paragraphs (a) to (j), a limited number of justification grounds, each with different requirements. Article XX can be relied on to justify measures that, amongst others:

- are necessary for the protection of public morals (Article XX(a));
- are necessary for the protection of the life or health of humans, animals or plants (Article XX(b));
- are necessary to secure compliance with national law, such as customs law, consumer protection law or intellectual property law, which is in itself not GATT-inconsistent (Article XX (d)); and
- relate to the 'conservation of exhaustible natural resources' (Article XX(g)).

WTO Members cannot rely on justification grounds other than those listed in Article XX. Note, however, that the listed grounds are quite broad. The Appellate Body has yet to rule on whether measures that aim to protect one of the listed societal values or interests *outside* the territorial jurisdiction of the Member taking the measure can be justified under Article XX of the GATT 1994. There is no *explicit* jurisdictional limitation in Article XX, but it is an open question whether such a jurisdictional limitation can be implied.

In *US – Shrimp (1998)*, a case involving a United States import ban on shrimp harvested in a way that resulted in the incidental killing of sea turtles, the Appellate Body noted that sea turtles migrate to or traverse waters subject to the United States' jurisdiction and thus that there was a 'sufficient nexus' between the sea turtles and the territorial jurisdiction of the United States for purposes of Article XX.

The most important justification grounds are discussed next.

4.2.1 Article XX(a) of the GATT 1994

For a GATT-inconsistent measure to be provisionally justified under Article XX(a):

- the policy objective pursued by the measure must be the protection of public morals; and
- the measure must be necessary to fulfil that policy objective.

With regard to the first condition, it has been held (in line with prior case law on the public morals exception in Article XIV(a) of the GATS) that the term 'public morals' denotes standards of right and wrong conduct maintained by or on behalf of a community or nation. The content of the concept of 'public morals' can differ from Member to Member, depending on factors such as prevailing social, cultural, ethical and religious values. Members thus have some scope to define and apply for themselves this concept in their territories according to their own systems and scales of values.

The deferential approach to the concept of 'public morals' just mentioned was followed in *EC – Seal Products (2014)*. The measure at issue in that case, referred to as the EU Seal Regime, was the European Union's prohibition on importation and marketing of seal products except where they were (1) derived from hunts by Inuit or other indigenous communities, (2) derived from

> hunts conducted for marine resource management pur-
> poses, or (3) imported for the personal use of travellers.
> The European Union argued that its Seal Regime was
> adopted to address EU public moral concerns regarding
> the welfare of seals. The panel agreed that these concerns
> fell within the scope of the concept of 'public morals'
> under Article XX(a) of the GATT 1994. The Appellate
> Body upheld the panel's finding that the EU public's
> concerns regarding seal welfare qualified as public moral
> concerns within the meaning of Article XX(a).

It is not always easy to identify the policy objective of a
measure in order to determine whether the measure is aimed at
the protection of public morals. Although a Member's articulation of the objective(s) of the measure at issue should be taken
into account, a panel is not bound by this and must take
account of all evidence put before it in this regard, including
the texts of statutes, legislative history and other evidence
regarding the structure and operation of the measure.

Finally, note that each Member has the right to determine the level of protection of public morals that it considers
appropriate and, therefore, that Members may set different
levels of protection even when responding to similar interests
of moral concern.

> In *EC – Seal Products (2014)*, the Appellate Body ruled
> that the fact that the European Union set different levels
> of protection with regard to animal welfare in relation to
> seal hunts than with regard to animal welfare in relation

to EU slaughterhouses or terrestrial wildlife hunts was irrelevant to the question whether the EU Seal Regime was a measure designed 'to protect public morals' within the meaning of Article XX(a) of the GATT 1994.

The second element of the Article XX(a) test, namely that the measure is 'necessary' to protect public morals, is more problematic. First of all, it is important to note that the question is not whether the policy objective aimed at by the Member or the level of protection of public morals it wishes to provide is necessary. The question is only whether the measure at issue is necessary to protect public morals at the level it has set.

According to well-established case law of the Appellate Body, the determination of whether a measure is necessary entails weighing and balancing the following three factors against each other:

- the importance of the societal value pursued by the measure at issue;
- the impact of the measure at issue on trade (an import prohibition is more trade restrictive than a labelling obligation); and
- the extent to which the measure at issue contributes to the protection or promotion of the value at stake.

The more important the societal value protected by the measure at issue, the more it contributes to its objective; and the less trade restrictive the measure, the easier the measure at issue may be considered to be necessary.

As held by the Appellate Body in *China - Publications and Audiovisual Products (2010)*, 'if a Member chooses to adopt a very restrictive measure, it will have to ensure that the measure is carefully designed so that the other elements to be taken into account in weighing and balancing the factors relevant to an assessment of the "necessity" of the measure will "outweigh" such restrictive effect'.

A preliminary conclusion (from the just described weighing and balancing test) that the measure is necessary must be confirmed by comparing the measure at issue with alternative measures. If a reasonably available alternative measure exists that is less trade restrictive while providing an equivalent contribution to the achievement of the measure's objective, the measure at issue will not be found to be necessary. It is established case law that it is the complaining Member that bears the burden of identifying possible alternative measures that the responding Member could have taken. It is, however, for the responding Member to show that any alternative measure identified by the complaining Member is not reasonably available, is not less trade restrictive and/or provides a lesser contribution to the achievement of the measure's objective. According to well-established case law, an alternative measure may be found *not* to be reasonably available where it is merely theoretical in nature (e.g. where the responding Member is not capable of taking it) or where the measure imposes an undue financial or technical burden on that Member.

In *EC – Seal Products (2014)*, Canada and Norway proposed that an alternative measure for the EU Seal Regime was market access for seal products that would be conditioned on compliance with animal welfare standards and certification and labelling requirements. The panel considered this alternative measure not to be reasonably available as even the most stringent certification system, which would be difficult to implement and enforce, would lead to increased numbers of inhumanely killed seals. Making the seal welfare standards or the certification and labelling requirements more lenient would make the alternative measure more reasonably available but would not meaningfully contribute to addressing EU public's moral concerns regarding seal welfare. The proposed measure was therefore not found to be an alternative measure for purposes of the 'necessity' requirement of Article XX(a). The Appellate Body upheld the panel's finding.

4.2.2 *Article XX(b) of the GATT 1994*

For a GATT-inconsistent measure to be provisionally justified under Article XX(b):

- the policy objective pursued by the measure must be the protection of the life or health of humans, animals or plants; and
- the measure must be necessary to fulfil that policy objective.

The first condition is relatively easy to meet. To determine whether a measure has been designed to achieve a health policy objective, the express provisions, design and structure of the measure at issue must be considered. Article XX(b) covers not only public health policy measures but also some environmental policy measures. However, to justify environmental policy measures, the existence not just of risks to 'the environment' generally, but specifically of risks to human, animal or plant life or health must be established.

> In the case *EC – Asbestos (2001)*, the measure at issue, a French ban on the importation and sale of asbestos and asbestos-containing products was clearly aimed at the protection of public health. In *Brazil – Retreaded Tyres (2007)*, Brazil argued that its import prohibition on retreaded tyres aimed to protect 'human health and the environment' against risks arising from the accumulation of waste tyres, which form fertile breeding grounds for disease-carrying mosquitoes and are highly combustible. The panel noted that Brazil used the term 'environment' to refer to animal and plant life or health. It found that Brazil had demonstrated the existence of risks to human, animal and plant life or health from toxic emissions caused by tyre fires as well as from dengue, a mosquito-borne disease, associated with the accumulation of waste tyres. It thus found that Brazil had established risks not only to the environment generally but to human, animal and plant health specifically.

With regard to the second requirement, namely, that the measure is necessary to protect the health of humans, animals or plants, please refer to the 'necessity' analysis in the context of Article XX(a) set out earlier (see Section 4.2.1). The same analysis applies to determine whether a measure is 'necessary' under Article XX(b). It is useful to recall that WTO Members are free to determine the *level* of protection of the relevant objective that they consider appropriate. It is the necessity of the measure, not of the level of protection, that is at issue under this requirement.

> In *EC – Asbestos (2001)*, the Appellate Body found that the French ban on the importation and sale of asbestos and asbestos-containing products was necessary to ensure the level of public health protection (a 'zero risk' level) chosen by France. Canada, the complainant in this case, argued that the 'controlled use' of asbestos and asbestos-containing products was an alternative measure that was less trade restrictive but would be just as effective in protecting public health. The Appellate Body did not agree with Canada because 'controlled use' entailed a significant residual risk and thus would not achieve France's 'zero risk' level of protection.

4.2.3 *Article XX(d) of the GATT 1994*

Another frequently used ground of justification is that contained in Article XX(d) of the GATT 1994. For a measure to be provisionally justified under Article XX(d):

- the measure must be designed to secure compliance with national laws or regulations, which, in themselves, are not GATT-inconsistent; and
- the measure must be necessary to ensure such compliance.

Regarding the first requirement, Article XX(d) gives examples of the kind of laws and regulations concerned. It explicitly refers to customs legislation, laws for the protection of intellectual property rights and laws for the protection of consumers against deceptive practices. It is important that these national laws or regulations, with which the measure at issue ensures compliance, must be consistent with the GATT 1994. Furthermore, the measure must contribute to securing compliance with national law; it is not required that the measure be guaranteed to achieve its objective with absolute certainty. Nor is use of coercion a necessary component of such a measure. Note also that the measure at issue does not need to be imposed exclusively to ensure compliance; it is sufficient if this is one of the reasons to impose the measure.

In *EC - Trademarks and Geographical Indications (2005)*, the European Union wanted to use the exception in Article XX(d) to justify measures imposed to ensure compliance with Regulation 2081/92. The panel, however, found this Regulation not to be GATT-consistent and thus concluded that the European Union could not make use of the Article XX(d) exception.

Regarding the second requirement, namely, the necessity of the measure at issue to ensure compliance with national laws, please refer to the 'necessity' analysis in the context of Article XX(a) set out earlier (see Section 4.2.1). The same analysis applies to determine whether a measure is 'necessary' under Article XX(d).

4.2.4 *Article XX(g) of the GATT 1994*

This exception is important because, together with Article XX(b), it offers WTO Members the possibility to take measures for the protection of the environment. A measure must meet three requirements in order to be provisionally justified under Article XX(g):

- the policy objective of the measure must be the 'conservation of exhaustible natural resources';
- the measure must 'relate to' this policy objective; and
- the measure must be made effective 'in conjunction with' restrictions on domestic production or consumption.

According to the Appellate Body in *China – Raw Materials (2012)*, 'conservation' means 'the preservation of the environment, especially of natural resources'. The precise contours of 'conservation' depend on the exhaustible natural resource at issue and are affected by the principle of permanent sovereignty over natural resources. Whereas the term 'exhaustible natural resources' brings to mind things like oil, gas, coal and minerals (and was undoubtedly also understood in this way in the late 1940s when the GATT was negotiated), this term has been interpreted by the Appellate Body in a broad, evolutionary manner to include not only minerals and other non-living resources, but also living resources, and, in particular, endangered species.

In *US – Shrimp (1998)*, the Appellate Body noted that the text of Article XX(g) was drafted more than fifty years ago and that it must be interpreted in the light of present conditions. The case concerned an import prohibition on shrimp that were caught in nets in which sea turtles often got entangled and consequently died. The Appellate Body remarked that during the past decennia, it had become clear that living species, though in principle capable of reproduction and in that sense 'renewable', are in practice susceptible to depletion and may be threatened by extinction, or, in other words, are 'exhaustible'. Referring to the objectives of the WTO as contained in the preamble to the WTO Agreement, and in particular the objective of sustainable development, as well as to multilateral environment agreements, the Appellate Body found that the term 'exhaustible natural resources' also includes living resources such as sea turtles. Therefore, Article XX(g) may be relied on in respect of a measure aimed at the protection of sea turtles.

The second condition for the use of Article XX(g) is that the measure at issue must 'relate to' the conservation of natural resources. It is clear that to 'relate to' is not the same as to 'be necessary for' (see Section 4.2.1). According to well-established case law, a measure 'relates to' the conservation of exhaustible natural resources if the relationship between the means (i.e. the measure) and the end (i.e. the conservation of exhaustible resources) is a real and close one. The measure may also not be disproportionately wide in its scope and reach in relation to the policy objective pursued.

> In *US – Shrimp (1998)*, the United States' measure required the use of a specific type of net that would prevent the entrapment of sea turtles. The Appellate Body concluded that this measure was related to the objective, namely, the protection of sea turtles, and that the measure was not disproportionate. The Appellate Body noted that the United States had not simply prohibited all shrimp imports but that the measure imposed requirements with regard to the mode of harvesting of the imported shrimp.

The third condition, namely, that the measure must be made effective 'in conjunction with' restrictions on domestic production or consumption, was interpreted by the Appellate Body as a requirement of 'even-handedness' in the imposition of restrictions on imported and domestic products. Article XX(g) does not demand that domestic and imported products are given the same treatment, but that measures related to the protection of exhaustible natural resources must be imposed on both groups of products. In other words, the 'burden' of measures taken to preserve exhaustible natural resources may not only weigh on imported products, but also must be spread over imported and domestic products. The Appellate Body in *China – Raw Materials (2012)* clarified that the phrase 'made effective in conjunction with' does not require a separate showing that the purpose of the measure at issue must be to make effective restrictions on domestic production or consumption. Instead, what is required is that the measure at issue 'work[s] together with restrictions on domestic production or consumption, which operate so as to conserve an exhaustible natural resource'.

> In *US – Shrimp (1998)*, the Appellate Body held that the measure at issue complied with this third condition because the United States did not prohibit only imported shrimp caught by harvesting methods that were sea turtle unfriendly, but also prohibited American shrimp trawlers from using these types of harvesting methods.

4.2.5 Article XX of the GATT 1994, other paragraphs

In addition to Articles XX(a), (b), (d) and (g) of the GATT 1994, also Articles XX(e) and (f) must be briefly mentioned. Article XX(e) of the GATT 1994 concerns measures 'relating to' the products of prison labour. Article XX(f) concerns measures 'imposed for' the protection of national treasures of artistic, historic or archaeological value. There is no relevant case law on either provision.

4.2.6 The chapeau of Article XX of the GATT 1994

Measures provisionally justified under one of the exceptions of Article XX (a) to (j) must subsequently meet the requirements of the chapeau of Article XX. The object and purpose of the chapeau is to prevent the application of the provisionally justified measures from constituting a misuse or abuse of the exceptions of Article XX. The interpretation and application of the chapeau in a particular case is a search for the appropriate line of equilibrium between the right of Members to adopt and maintain trade-restrictive measures that pursue certain legitimate societal values, on the one hand, and the right of other Members to market access and non-discriminatory treatment, on the other. The requirements set out in the chapeau do not apply to the measure itself but to the manner in which the measure is applied.

According to the chapeau, the application of the provisionally justified measure may not constitute:

- arbitrary or unjustifiable discrimination between countries where the same conditions prevail; or
- a disguised restriction on international trade.

The requirements imposed by the chapeau have been highly relevant in dispute settlement practice, and several of the most controversial decisions by panels and the Appellate Body have turned on these requirements.

When a measure is applied without any regard for the difference in conditions between countries and/or this measure is applied in a rigid and inflexible manner, the application of the measure may constitute 'arbitrary discrimination' within the meaning of the chapeau of Article XX.

The application of the measure at issue in *US - Shrimp (1998)* was found to constitute arbitrary discrimination by the Appellate Body because the United States applied this measure in a very rigid and inflexible manner and without any regard for the conditions in the exporting country. It required that countries applying for certification to export shrimp to the United States adopt a comprehensive regulatory programme to protect sea turtles that was essentially the same as the United States' program without inquiring into the appropriateness of that programme for the conditions prevailing in the exporting countries. In order to comply with the Appellate Body's ruling, the United States modified its measure to require that countries adopt a programme comparable in effectiveness to the US programme. When this amended measure was challenged in *US - Shrimp (Article 21.5 - Malaysia) (2001)*, the panel found that conditioning market access on the adoption of a programme *comparable in effectiveness* allows for sufficient flexibility in the application of the measure so as to avoid 'arbitrary discrimination'. The Appellate Body agreed.

The application of a measure may be found to constitute 'unjustifiable discrimination' if the discrimination should have been *foreseen* and was *not merely inadvertent or unavoidable*. One factor that may contribute to a finding of unjustifiable discrimination is a failure to make serious efforts, in good faith, to negotiate a multilateral solution before resorting to unilateral measures.

In *US – Shrimp (1998)*, the application of the US measure was found to constitute unjustifiable discrimination because the United States imposed unilateral trade-restrictive measures to protect sea turtles without first attempting to reach the same objective by negotiating a multilateral agreement.

According to well-established case law, the analysis of whether discrimination is 'arbitrary or unjustifiable' within the meaning of the chapeau can be established by looking at the *cause* or *rationale* of the discrimination. The main question is then whether the discrimination can be reconciled with or is rationally related to the policy objective with respect to which the measure has been provisionally justified under one of the subparagraphs of Article XX.

In *EC – Seal Products (2014)*, the Appellate Body concluded that the measure at issue, the EU Seal Regime, which was provisionally justified under Article XX(a), was applied in a manner that constituted arbitrary or unjustifiable discrimination, for three reasons. First, the distinction in the EU Seal Regime between seal products derived from hunts by indigenous communities (which were allowed on the EU market) and those derived from commercial hunts (which were banned) could not be

reconciled with the objective of addressing the EU public's moral concerns regarding seal welfare because both
types of hunts seriously affected seal welfare. Second, due
to ambiguities in the indigenous community exception,
seal products derived from what should in fact be properly characterized as commercial hunts could potentially
enter the EU market under this exception, further undermining the objective of the measure. Third, the EU had
not made comparable efforts to facilitate the access of the
Canadian Inuit to the indigenous community exception
as it did with respect to the Greenlandic Inuit.

Finally, note that the relevant 'conditions' in the
phrase *'between countries where the same conditions prevail"*
in the chapeau of Article XX should be understood by reference to the applicable subparagraph of Article XX under
which the measure was provisionally justified and the substantive obligations under the GATT 1994 with which a violation has been found. A respondent that considers that the
relevant conditions prevailing in different countries are not
'the same' bears the burden to prove this.

In *EC – Seal Products (2014)*, the Appellate Body examined whether the European Union had shown that the
'conditions' prevailing in the Members compared for
purposes of the finding of violation of Article I of the
GATT 1994 – Canada and Norway, on the one hand, and
in Greenland, on the other hand – were relevantly different. In its assessment, the Appellate Body referred to

conditions relevant to the public morals concern regarding the welfare of seals under which the EC Seal Regime was provisionally justified. It noted that the European Union had not demonstrated that the animal welfare conditions related to seal hunts in Canada and Norway were different from those in Greenland. Consequently, the Appellate Body assumed the relevant 'conditions' prevailing in Greenland to be the same as those in Canada and Norway.

A measure which is provisionally justified under Article XX will be considered to constitute 'a disguised restriction on international trade' if the design, architecture or structure of the measure at issue reveals that this measure does in fact not pursue the legitimate policy objectives on which the provisional justification was based but, in fact, pursues trade-restrictive (i.e. protectionist) objectives.

4.3 General exceptions under Article XIV of the GATS

Like the GATT 1994, the GATS also provides for a 'general exceptions' provision allowing Members to deviate, under certain conditions, from their obligations under the GATS. The similarities between Article XX of the GATT 1994 and Article XIV of the GATS are striking. However, there are also differences. Under Article XIV (a) to (e) of the GATS, WTO Members can justify otherwise GATS-inconsistent measures that are, amongst others:

- necessary to protect public morals or to maintain public order (Article XIV(a));
- necessary to protect human, animal or plant life or health (Article XIV(b)); or
- necessary to secure compliance with laws or regulations that are not inconsistent with the GATS (Article XIV(c)).

A WTO Member may also rely on Article XIV of the GATS to justify measures that:

- are inconsistent with Article XVII of the GATS (i.e. the national treatment obligation), when the difference in treatment is aimed at the equitable and effective imposition or collection of direct taxes (Article XIV(d)); or
- are inconsistent with Article II of the GATS (i.e. the MFN treatment obligation), when the difference in treatment results from an international agreement on the avoidance of double taxation (Article XIV(e)).

Article XIV of the GATS, just like Article XX of the GATT 1994, embodies a two-tier test. In order to determine whether a measure can be justified under Article XIV of the GATS, one must determine, first, whether the measure can provisionally be justified under one of the specific exceptions of paragraphs (a) to (e) of Article XIV, and, if so, second, whether the application of this measure meets the requirements of the chapeau of Article XIV.

The case law on Article XIV of the GATS is currently limited. However, due to the similarity in the language, the case law under Article XX of the GATT 1994 is relevant for the interpretation of Article XIV of the GATS.

4.3.1 Article XIV(a) of the GATS

Article XIV(a) sets out a two-tier test to determine whether an otherwise GATS-inconsistent measure is provisionally justified under this provision. The Member invoking this exception must show that:

- the policy objective pursued by the measure at issue is the protection of public morals or the maintenance of public order; and
- the measure is necessary to achieve that objective.

With regard to the first requirement, case law has clarified that what relates to 'public morals' or 'public order' can vary in time and space, depending on a range of factors including prevailing social, cultural, ethical and religious values. Thus, it is recognized that Members should be given some scope to define and apply these concepts for themselves in their territories 'according to their own systems and scales of values'.

The term 'public morals' has been defined as 'standards of right and wrong conduct maintained by or on behalf of a community or nation', whereas the term 'public order' has been defined as 'the preservation of the fundamental interests of a society, as reflected in public policy and law'. According to footnote 5 to Article XIV(a), a Member can only invoke the 'public order' exception when there is a genuine and sufficiently serious threat to one of the fundamental interests of society, such as standards of law, security and morality. The concepts 'public morals' and 'public order' may partially overlap with each other.

In *US – Gambling (2005)*, Antigua and Barbuda challenged the GATS-consistency of a number of US federal and state laws that prohibit the remote supply of gambling and betting services, including Internet gambling. The United States, *inter alia*, argued that this form of gambling posed risks with regard to organized crime, fraud and money laundry practices, underage gambling and gambling addiction. Therefore, according to the United States, the measures at issue could be justified under Article XIV(a) of the GATS as necessary to protect public morals and maintain public order. The panel and the Appellate Body readily recognized the prohibition on remote gambling services as a measure taken to protect public morals and maintain public order.

Regarding the second requirement, namely, whether the measure is necessary to protect public morals or public order, please refer to the well-established case law on Articles XX(a), (b) and XX(d) of the GATT 1994, discussed in Section 4.2.1.

In *US – Gambling (2005)*, the panel had found that the US measures were not 'necessary' because, in rejecting Antigua and Barbuda's invitation to engage in bilateral or multilateral consultations, the United States had failed to explore and exhaust reasonably available WTO-consistent alternatives to the measures at issue. The Appellate Body disagreed with the panel's 'necessity' analysis because it did *not* focus on an alternative measure that was reasonably available to the United States to achieve the stated objectives. Engaging in consultations with Antigua and Barbuda was not an appropriate alternative for the panel to consider because consultations are 'by definition a process, the results of which are uncertain and therefore not capable of comparison with the measures at issue in this case'.

4.3.2 *Article XIV(c) of the GATS*

Article XIV(c) can be used as a ground for justification of an otherwise GATS-inconsistent measure if:

- the measure has been designed to secure compliance with national laws or regulations;
- the national laws and regulations concerned are not inconsistent with the GATS; and
- the measure at issue is necessary to ensure compliance with those national laws and regulations.

Article XIV(c) gives three non-exhaustive examples of such laws or regulations, namely, those relating to (1) the prevention of deceptive and fraudulent practices, (2) the protection of the privacy of individuals and (3) safety.

The requirements for the use of Article XIV(c) as justification are largely similar to the requirements for the use of Article XX(d) of the GATT 1994. It is therefore not surprising that in *US – Gambling (2005)*, the panel and the Appellate Body had recourse to case law on Article XX(d) of the GATT 1994 for the interpretation of Article XIV(c) of the GATS (see Section 4.2.3).

4.3.3 Article XIV of the GATS, other paragraphs

In addition to Article XIV(a) and (c) of the GATS, Article XIV(b), (d) and (e) deserve a brief mention. Article XIV(b) provides an general exception for measures *necessary* to protect human, animal or plant life or health. There is no case law to date on this provision, but, due to the similarity in the language, the case law on Article XX(b) of the GATT is of relevance to its interpretation.

By contrast, the exceptions in Article XIV(d) and (e) of the GATS do not have an counterpart in Article XX of the GATT 1994. They are specific to the GATS. Article XIV(d) as well as (e) have a rather narrow scope. The grounds of justification, set out in these provisions for measures aimed at ensuring the equitable or effective imposition or collection of direct taxes (Article XIV(d)) and for measures resulting from an agreement on the avoidance of double taxation (Article XIV(e)), *only* justify inconsistency with the national treatment obligation of Article XVII of the GATS *or* the MFN treatment obligation of Article II of the GATS, respectively. There is no case law on either of these provisions.

4.3.4 The chapeau of Article XIV of the GATS

In the same way as the chapeau of Article XX of the GATT 1994, the chapeau of Article XIV of the GATS requires that the application of the measure at issue does not constitute:

- arbitrary or unjustifiable discrimination between countries where the same conditions prevail; or
- a disguised restriction on trade in services.

The interpretation and application of these requirements are the same as those of Article XX of the GATT 1994. A lack of consistency in the application of the measure at issue might lead to the conclusion that 'arbitrary or unjustifiable discrimination' or a 'disguised restriction on trade' are present.

In *US – Gambling*, the panel found that it was unclear whether the US Interstate Horseracing Act allowed certain forms of remote gambling on horse races in the United States. This pointed towards a lack of consistency in the application of the prohibition on remote gambling services because the supply of these services by foreign providers was clearly prohibited. The panel therefore concluded that the United States had not shown that the measure at issue (the prohibition on the remote supply of gambling services) was applied in a way that did not constitute arbitrary or unjustifiable discrimination or a disguised restriction to trade in services. The Appellate Body agreed.

4.4 Exceptions for national and international security

The GATT 1994 in Article XXI and the GATS in Article XIV *bis* provide for exceptions relating to national and international security. According to these Articles, WTO Members may take measures that are otherwise GATT- or GATS-inconsistent in order to protect national or international peace and security.

Article XXI(a) of the GATT 1994 and Article XIV*bis* (a) of the GATS permit a Member to withhold information that it would normally be required to supply when it 'considers' disclosure of that information 'contrary to its essential security interests'.

More generally, Article XXI(b) of the GATT 1994 and Article XIV*bis* (b) of the GATS allow a Member to take any action it 'considers necessary' for the protection of its essential security interests:

- relating to fissionable materials;
- relating to trade in arms or in other materials, or the provision of services, directly or indirectly, for military use; or
- taken in times of war or other emergency in international relations.

Furthermore, under Article XXI(c) of the GATT 1994 and Article XIV*bis* (c) of the GATS, WTO Members are also allowed to take GATT- or GATS-inconsistent measures

- to comply with their obligations under the United Nations Charter for the maintenance of international peace and security (e.g. economic sanctions imposed by the UN Security Council).

Article XXI of the GATT was at issue in a few disputes under the GATT 1947, but neither Article XXI of the GATT 1994 nor Article XIV *bis* of the GATS have been the subject of

111

panel or Appellate Body rulings to date. It is still an open question to what extent the use by Members of these exceptions to justify otherwise GATT- or GATS-inconsistent measures is 'justiciable' (i.e. is susceptible to control by the WTO dispute settlement organs). The security exceptions of Article XXI of the GATT 1994 and Article XIV *bis* of the GATS are formulated in a manner that leaves a lot of discretion to WTO Members. Furthermore, unlike the general exceptions under Article XX of the GATT 1994 and Article XIV of the GATS, these security exceptions are not subject to the requirements of a chapeau to avoid their misuse by WTO Members (see Sections 4.2.6 and 4.3.4).

4.5 Exceptions for safeguard measures

WTO law also provides for economic emergency exceptions. These exceptions are set out in Article XIX of the GATT 1994 and the Agreement on Safeguards (regarding safeguard measures) as well as Articles XII and XVIII:B of the GATT 1994 and Article XII of the GATS (regarding balance of payment measures). This Section deals with the exceptions for safeguard measures. The exceptions for balance of payments measures are addressed in Section 4.6.

Article XIX of the GATT 1994 and the Agreement on Safeguards allow Members to adopt otherwise WTO–inconsistent measures referred to as 'safeguard measures' in situations where a surge in imports causes or threatens to cause serious injury to the domestic industry. Safeguard measures are not provided for under the GATS, but the possibility to 'complete' the GATS on this issue in the future through multilateral negotiations has been explicitly left open (see Article X of the GATS).

When a WTO Member wants to take a safeguard measure, the strict requirements of Article XIX of the GATT 1994 and the Agreement on Safeguards must be met. The reason for the strictness of these requirements is that safeguard measures are applied to fair trade. The exporter is 'blameless'; the imported products are not being dumped nor are they being subsidized (see Sections 5.2 and 5.3). Instead, the imported products are 'only' so competitive that they oust the domestic products from the market.

According to the Appellate Body in *US – Line Pipe (2002)*, there is a 'natural tension between, on the one hand, defining the appropriate and legitimate scope of the right to apply safeguard measures and, on the other hand, ensuring that safeguard measures are not applied against "fair trade" beyond what is necessary to provide extraordinary and temporary relief'. The Agreement on Safeguards aims to balance the right of a Member to apply safeguard measures against the need to protect the multilateral integrity of ongoing trade concessions.

There are three categories of rules that apply to safeguard measures, namely, rules relating to:

• the substantive requirements that must be fulfilled in order to take a safeguard measure;

113

- the procedural requirements at the national and international level that a WTO Member must meet when taking a safeguard measure; and
- the characteristics of safeguard measures.

4.5.1 *Substantive requirements*

As provided in Article XIX of the GATT 1994 and Article 2 of the Agreement on Safeguards, safeguard measures may only be applied when three requirements are met, namely:

- there are increased imports;
- there is 'serious injury' or threat thereof to the domestic industry; and
- there is a causal link between the increased imports and the serious injury.

4.5.1.1 Increased imports

Safeguard measures may only be applied exceptionally in an economic *emergency*. Therefore, they cannot be applied as a response to just any increase in imports. Instead, the required increase in imports must be recent, sudden, sharp and significant. Both the rate (e.g. 70 per cent) and the amount of increase (e.g. 100 000 units) must be considered, and the import trends over the entire investigation period must be assessed. Furthermore, the increase in imports must be a result of 'unforeseen developments' (see Article XIX of the GATT 1994). In this way, it is determined whether the situation is in fact an emergency situation. If the increase in imports took place some time ago, has been taking place for an extended period, is rather limited, or was foreseeable, then there is no emergency situation within the meaning of Article XIX of the GATT 1994 and the Agreement on Safeguards.

Examine Figures 4.1 and 4.2, showing the increase in smartphone imports in Industria and Agricola during the investigation period 2013–15. In both examples, there is an increase in imports in the investigation period. The amount of increase (20 000 units to 80 000 units), as well as the rate of increase (300 per cent), is quite significant in both cases. However, if one looks at the import trends, it is clear that, in Industria, there has been a recent, sudden and sharp increase in smartphone imports within the meaning of the Agreement on Safeguards. It is doubtful whether the same conclusion can be reached with respect to the increase of imports in Agricola.

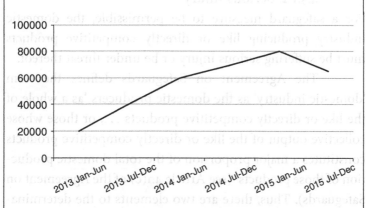

Figure 4.1: Smartphone imports into Agricola

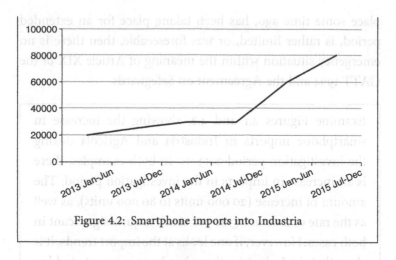

Figure 4.2: Smartphone imports into Industria

The required increase in imports does not need to be an increase in absolute terms; it is sufficient that there is an increase in imports compared to domestic production – in other words, a relative increase.

4.5.1.2 Serious injury

For a safeguard measure to be permissible, the domestic industry producing like or directly competitive products must be suffering serious injury or be under threat thereof.

The Agreement on Safeguards defines the term 'domestic industry' as the domestic producers 'as a whole of the like or directly competitive products . . ., or those whose collective output of the like or directly competitive products constitutes a major proportion of the total domestic production of those products' (see Article 4.1(c) of the Agreement on Safeguards). Thus, there are two elements to the determination of the relevant 'domestic industry':

- it must produce 'like or directly competitive products' to those being imported in increased quantities; and
- its production must constitute the entirety or a major proportion of the domestic production of such products.

Although there is no definition of what constitutes a 'major proportion' of total domestic production, according to established case law it is not required that the relevant producers account for the majority of domestic production. What is a 'major proportion' will depend on the specific circumstances of the case.

There has recently been a surge of imports of smartphones with touchscreens into Industria. PhoneHouse and E-Phone, two Industrian smartphone producers, account for 45 per cent of smartphone production in Industria. The remaining production of smartphones in Industria is in the hands of a number of small producers. Industrian smartphone producers produce mainly smartphones with keypads, which have been shown to be directly competitive with smartphones with touchscreens in the Industrian market. PhoneHouse and E-Phone may be regarded as the relevant 'domestic industry' for purposes of the determination of 'serious injury' under Article 4 of the Agreement on Safeguards.

As stated earlier, for a safeguard measure to be permissible, the domestic industry concerned must be suffering serious injury or be under threat thereof. The required 'serious injury' exists when there is a significant overall impairment in the position of the relevant domestic industry (see Article 4.1(a) of the Agreement on Safeguards). 'Serious injury' is a stricter requirement than the requirement of 'material injury', which applies for the imposition of an anti-dumping measure or a countervailing measure (see Sections 5.2.2 and 5.3.3). This is not surprising because a safeguard measure is applied to fair trade, whereas an anti-dumping measure or a countervailing measure is applied to unfair trade. A 'threat of serious injury' is defined as 'serious injury that is clearly imminent', meaning that the anticipated 'serious injury' must be on the verge of occurring and that there must be a 'very high degree of likelihood that the threat will materialise in the very near future'.

To determine whether there is serious injury or a threat thereof, the following factors must be considered, among others:

- the rate and amount of the increase in imports of the product at issue, in absolute and relative terms;
- the share of the domestic market taken by increased imports; and
- changes in the level of sales, production, productivity, capacity utilization, profits and losses of, and employment in the domestic industry.

This list of factors is not exhaustive. All factors having a bearing on the situation of the domestic industry can and must be examined. It is not required, however, that all factors point towards 'serious injury'. Even when some factors do not point towards 'serious injury', a WTO Member can still conclude that the domestic industry is suffering from or under threat of serious injury.

4.5.1.3 Causation

The third and last substantive requirement for the application of a safeguard measure is the 'causation' requirement, set out in Article 4.2(b) of the Agreement on Safeguards. The test for establishing 'causation' is twofold:

- a demonstration of the causal link between the 'increased imports' and the 'serious injury' or threat thereof (the 'causal link' element); and
- an identification of any injury caused by factors other than the increased imports and the non-attribution of this injury to these imports (the 'non-attribution' element).

The 'causal link' requirement entails 'a genuine and substantial relationship of cause and effect' between the injury and the increased imports. Note that it is not necessary to show that the increased imports alone are the cause of the injury suffered by the domestic industry. However, the injury that is caused by other factors (such as technological developments and decreasing customer demand for the product at issue) may not be attributed to the increase in imports.

Industria's domestic smartphone industry has seen its market share rapidly decrease and its profitability drop in a period that coincides with a sudden, sharp increase in smartphone imports. However, in this same period, a surge in the subscription rates of telecom providers has led to decreased smartphone use in Industria and, consequently, fewer smartphone purchases. In addition, the failure of PhoneHouse and E-Phone to keep up with new technologies that significantly increase the battery life of smartphones has led many Industrian consumers to switch to phones made by more technologically advanced smartphone producers. Finally, government regulations in Industria that require domestic smartphone producers to incorporate special screens to minimize the negative health effects of prolonged exposure to radiation from smartphones have drastically increased production costs for Industrian producers. Industrian authorities conducting the safeguard investigation will have to distinguish and separate the injurious effects of these three 'other' factors from the injurious effects of the increased imports in order to ensure that 'the final determination of causation rests, properly, on the genuine and substantial relationship of cause and effect between increased imports and serious injury'.

4.5.2 *Procedural requirements*

To establish whether the substantive requirements for safeguard measures have been met, the competent authorities of the relevant WTO Member must conduct an investigation. Article 3 of the Agreement on Safeguards sets out procedural requirements that these competent authorities must meet when conducting such investigation. In this respect, it is important that all interested parties are offered the opportunity to be heard by the competent authorities and that these authorities publish a detailed report containing all their findings and conclusions concerning the substantive requirements for the imposition of safeguard measures. If these procedural requirements are not met, the safeguard measure applied is in violation of WTO law. Article 12 of the Agreement on Safeguards further requires that a WTO Member wishing to take a safeguard measure immediately notify the WTO Committee on Safeguards of all decisions concerning the safeguard measure (such as the decision to start an investigation, the decision to apply a safeguard measure and the decision to extend a safeguard measure). The WTO Member concerned must make all relevant information available to this WTO Committee and, in particular, provide a description of the product at issue, evidence of serious injury to the domestic industry caused by increased imports, a description of the proposed safeguard measure, the expected duration of the measure and the timetable for the progressive liberalization of the measure. The Member applying or extending a safeguard measure must provide adequate opportunity for prior consultations with other WTO Members that are affected by the measure.

4.5.3 Characteristics of safeguard measures

A safeguard measure is a measure that *temporarily* restricts import competition in order to give some 'breathing space' to the domestic industry to allow it to adapt to new market conditions. As stated earlier, it is an *extraordinary* remedy, applied in a situation of fair trade.

Safeguard measures typically take the form of customs duties above the binding or quantitative restrictions. Generally speaking, these measures conflict with, respectively, Article II and Article XI of the GATT 1994 (see Sections 3.2 and 3.4), but they can be justified under Article XIX of the GATT 1994 if they meet the requirements of this provision and the requirements of the Agreement on Safeguards.

4.5.3.1 Duration of a safeguard measure

A WTO Member may only apply a safeguard measure as long as it is necessary to remedy or prevent the injury or threat thereof and to give the domestic industry the opportunity to adjust (Article 7 of the Agreement on Safeguards).

The maximum initial duration of a safeguard measure is four years. It is possible to extend this duration, but only if:

- the measure continues to be necessary to remedy or prevent serious injury or threat thereof to the domestic industry and
- there is evidence that the domestic industry is adjusting.

The total duration of a safeguard measure, including extension, may not be longer than eight years, or ten years in the case of developing-country Members (Articles 7.3 and 9.2 of the Agreement on Safeguards). Once the import of a product has been subjected to a safeguard measure, this product may not be subjected to such a measure again for a period of time equal to the duration of the previously applied safeguard measure. Note that developing-country Members may apply a safeguard measure again on the same product sooner than developed-country Members.

> If Industria has imposed a safeguard measure in the form of a quantitative restriction on imports of smartphones for a period of six years, it cannot impose a new safeguard measure on smartphones during the six years following the termination of the previous safeguard measure.

Furthermore, the Agreement on Safeguards requires that every safeguard measure applied for a period longer than one year be progressively liberalized, meaning that it must be made gradually less trade restrictive. For a safeguard measure that is applied for a period of more than three years, the WTO Member applying the measure is obliged to carry out a mid-term review of whether the measure still meets the requirements for the imposition of a safeguard measure. If this is not the case, the WTO Member involved must withdraw the safeguard measure (or, in any case, speed up its progressive liberalization).

4.5.3.2 Extent of a safeguard measure

A safeguard measure may only be applied to the extent necessary to prevent or remedy the serious injury and to give the domestic industry the opportunity to adjust (see Article 5 of the Agreement on Safeguards). A safeguard measure that takes the form of a quota may not restrict imports to levels less than the average of the last three representative years unless a 'clear justification' for this is provided.

In addition, safeguard measures may only be applied to the extent that they address the serious injury (or threat thereof) *attributable to increased imports*. The share of the injury that was caused by 'other' factors may not be addressed by the safeguard measure.

4.5.3.3 Non-discrimination

A safeguard measure must be applied in a non-discriminatory manner, meaning it must be applied to all imports of the product at issue, regardless of origin (see Article 2 of the Agreement on Safeguards). Members are not allowed to apply safeguard measures selectively, for example, by only applying the measure to the import of the product from the source that is responsible for the surge of imports causing injury to the domestic industry.

> If the Industrian smartphone industry suffers serious injury as a consequence of massive importation of cheap Alpinian smartphones and Industria wants to take a safeguard measure to temporarily protect its smartphone industry by increasing the import duties on smartphones above the tariff binding, Industria must also impose the higher duties on all like or directly competitive smartphones of Agricolan origin, even if the imports of these smartphones have not increased.

Where the safeguard measure takes the form of a quota allocated among supplying countries, Article 5.2(a) of the Agreement on Safeguards provides for rules on the allocation of shares in the quota similar to those of Article XIII of the GATT 1994 (see Section 3.4.1).

4.5.3.4 Compensation

A safeguard measure is taken in a situation of fair trade and disturbs the negotiated balance of rights and obligations between Members. A WTO Member that takes a safeguard measure is therefore obliged to restore this balance. In order to do so, the Member must engage in consultations on compensation with those WTO Members having a substantial interest in exporting the product restricted by the safeguard measure (see Articles 8 and 12.3 of the Agreement on Safeguards). This compensation can, for example, be in the form of a decrease in import duties on other products of interest to the affected Members. The nature and extent of the compensation is negotiated between the WTO Members concerned. If no agreement on the compensation can be reached, the WTO Members whose export is being restricted may increase their import duties on products originating in the WTO Member imposing the safeguard measure or may otherwise restrict the importation of this Member's products to a 'substantially equivalent' level.

4.5.3.5 Provisional safeguard measures

As discussed earlier, in normal circumstances, an elaborate (and thus time-consuming) investigation must be carried out to determine whether all the substantive requirements to take a safeguard measure have been met. In 'critical circumstances', a WTO Member may take a provisional safeguard measure after a preliminary investigation (see Article 6 of the Agreement on Safeguards). Circumstances are regarded as critical if the delay in the application of the safeguard measure would cause damage that would be difficult to repair.

A provisional safeguard measure has a maximum duration of 200 days and can only take the form of an increase in customs duties. When a provisional safeguard measure has been imposed, a full-fledged investigation must still take place. If this investigation shows that the conditions for imposition of a safeguard measure are not met, the provisional measure lapses and the duties collected must be refunded.

4.5.4 Special safeguard measures

WTO Members can, or could, take special safeguard measures in specific cases. Article 5 of the Agreement on Agriculture allows for the imposition of a special safeguard measure limited to agricultural products under less strict requirements than those set out in the Agreement on Safeguards. This exemption from the market access rules of the Agreement on Agriculture has been found by the Appellate Body to be 'narrowly circumscribed' and limited to those WTO Members that have reserved their rights to use it. Note that Section 16 of the China Accession Protocol provided for a *transitional product-specific safeguard mechanism*, under which safeguard measures could be more easily imposed on Chinese exports than under the Agreement on Safeguards. However, this special safeguard mechanism expired at the end of 2013.

4.6 Exceptions for balance of payments measures

Another situation of economic emergency that may justify the use of measures that are otherwise inconsistent with the

GATT 1994 or the GATS is that of problems in a Member's balance of payments.

Articles XII and XVIII:B of the GATT 1994 and the Understanding on the Balance of Payments Provisions of the GATT 1994 (the Understanding on BoP Provisions) contain the rules that allow WTO Members to safeguard their external financial position and to protect their balance of payments by restricting the quantity or value of imported products.

Balance of payment measures can take the form of quantitative restrictions or price-based measures. Such measures may be inconsistent with Article II (in the case of price-based measures) or Article XI (in the case of quantitative restrictions) of the GATT 1994 (see Sections 3.2 and 3.4). However, Article XII justifies such measures under strict conditions. First, the balance of payments measure at issue may not exceed what is necessary to address the balance of payments problem at hand. Specifically, they should be limited to what is necessary 'to forestall the imminent threat of, or to stop, a serious decline in a Member's monetary reserves, or in the case of a [Member] with very low monetary reserves, to achieve a reasonable rate of increase in its reserves'. The determination of whether these criteria are present is based on statistical and other facts provided by the International Monetary Fund (IMF) (see Article XV of the GATT 1994). Second, balance of payments measures must avoid unnecessary damage to the commercial and economic interests of other Members. Third, these measures may only be applied on a temporary basis and must be progressively relaxed as the external financial situation improves.

In acknowledgement of the special position of developing countries, Article XVII:B of the GATT 1994 provides less onerous conditions for the imposition of balance of payments measures by developing country Members.

Whereas under Articles XII and XVIII:B of the GATT 1994 initially only balance of payments measures in the form of quantitative restrictions were allowed, under the Understanding on BoP Provisions WTO Members are now committed to give preference to 'price-based' measures (import surcharges, import deposit requirements or other equivalent trade measures with an impact on the price of imported goods).

Article XII:1 of the GATS contains very similar rules allowing Members, in situations of serious balance of payments problems and external financial difficulties or a threat thereof, to adopt or maintain balance of payments measures that restrict trade in services in a GATS-inconsistent manner. The IMF also plays a central role in providing the relevant data for establishing the consistency of balance of payments measures with the criteria of Article XII:1 of the GATS.

Balance of payments measures are reviewed by the WTO Committee on Balance-of-Payments Restrictions (BoP Committee) to determine their consistency with the GATT 1994 and the GATS. Panels reviewing the consistency of balance of payments measures should take into account the deliberations and conclusions of the BoP Committee.

Since the establishment of the WTO, limited use has been made of the balance of payments exceptions in Articles XII and XVIII:B of the GATT 1994 and Article XII of the GATS.

4.7 Exceptions for regional trade agreements

WTO law also provides for exceptions for 'regional trade agreements'. Article XXIV of the GATT 1994 (elaborated on further in the Understanding on Article XXIV) and Article V of the GATS allow WTO Members to liberalize trade more rapidly among a limited group of Members by means of regional trade agreements (RTAs), now also referred to as preferential trade agreements (PTAs). Although, originally, these groups of Members comprised countries in the same region (hence the use of the term 'regional trade agreements'), in recent years, the countries involved in economic integration efforts are often countries or groups of countries from different regions (hence the use of the term 'preferential trade agreements'). However, because the term 'regional trade agreements' is still used by WTO Members to refer to this type of agreement, it is used also in this book.

When WTO Members conclude a regional trade agreement to form a customs union or a free-trade area, they grant each other more favourable treatment in trade matters (such as the abolition of all customs duties) than they grant to WTO Members that are not part of that customs union or free-trade area. This conflicts with the MFN treatment obligation of Article I of the GATT 1994 and Article II of the GATS (see Sections 2.2 and 2.3). However, WTO law recognizes that trade liberalization pursued within regional trading blocs may serve as a stepping stone for trade liberalization at the multilateral level in future. Therefore, exceptions for regional trade agreements exist and can be relied on to justify a violation of the MFN treatment obligation (and possibly other obligations) under the GATT 1994 and the GATS.

In recent years, regional trade agreements have pro-liferated. In addition, some of the RTAs recently concluded or currently being negotiated are of unprecedented scope and pursue much deeper levels of economic integration than RTAs have done in the past. Currently, more than 260 regional trade agreements are in force between WTO Members. Well-known examples of such regional trade agreements are the recent Trans-Pacific Partnership (TPP) Agreement (among twelve Pacific Rim countries), the North American Free Trade Agreement (NAFTA), and the agreements establishing the Association of Southeast Asian Nations (ASEAN) Free Trade Area (AFTA), the Southern Common Market (MERCOSUR), the Common Market of the Caribbean (CARICOM), the Southern African Development Community (SADC), and the Common Market of Eastern and Southern Africa (COMESA). Negotiations on many other regional trade agreements, including the Transatlantic Trade and Investment Partnership (TTIP) negotiations (between the European Union and the United States), are ongoing. There is great concern that this large number of customs unions and free-trade areas (which by their nature discriminate against WTO Members that are not part of them) creates a 'spaghetti bowl' of overlapping preferential arrangements that forms a threat to the multilateral trading system, which is based on the principle of non-discrimination. However, as noted in a 2015 World Bank paper, '[d]espite the explosive increase in PTA adoption, the WTO estimates that overall, excluding (including) intra-EU trade, 84 per cent (70 per cent) of world merchandise trade still takes place on an MFN basis'.

Article XXIV of the GATT 1994 and Article V of the GATS set out the requirements that must be fulfilled for the use of the exceptions for regional trade agreements concerning trade in goods and trade in services, respectively. These requirements aim to ensure that regional trade agreements create more trade than they divert. When a regional integration agreement concerns trade in goods as well as in services, it must meet the requirements of both Articles.

4.7.1 Regional trade agreements on trade in goods

A measure otherwise inconsistent with the GATT 1994 is justified under Article XXIV:5 of the GATT 1994 when:

- the measure is introduced upon the formation of a customs union, a free-trade area or an interim agreement that meets all the requirements set out in WTO law (see below); and
- the formation of the customs union or free-trade area would be prevented (i.e. made impossible) if the introduction of the measure at issue were not allowed.

WTO Members can choose between forming a free-trade area or a customs union. In a free-trade area, there is less integration than in a customs union. In a customs union, internal trade is liberalized and the trade with third countries is jointly regulated, whereas only the internal trade is liberalized in a free-trade area. For customs unions as well as free-trade areas, the following is required:

- the elimination of import duties and other restrictions on 'substantially all trade' between the Members that are part of the customs union or free-trade area (the internal trade requirement); and
- that, as a consequence of the formation of the customs union or free-trade area, trade with third countries is not made more difficult or more restricted.

An additional requirement applies for a customs union, namely, that the import duties and other restrictive regulations of commerce that the customs union members apply to trade with third countries must be 'substantially the same' (the external trade requirement). Note that the word 'substantially' in the terms 'substantially all trade' and 'substantially the same' provides some flexibility, albeit limited, to Members in liberalizing their internal trade or creating a common external trade policy when forming a free-trade area or customs union.

In *Turkey – Textiles (1999)*, Turkey relied on Article XXIV to justify its imposition of quantitative restrictions on textiles from India. According to Turkey, without such restrictions, it would have been prevented from forming a customs union with the European Communities (EC). This was because the European Communities would otherwise have excluded textiles (which accounted for 40 per cent of Turkey's exports to the European Communities) from the European Communities–Turkey customs union in order to avoid circumvention of its own quantitative restrictions on textiles from India by importation via Turkey. Regarding the requirement on internal trade, the

Appellate Body noted, it is clear that 'substantially all the trade' is not the same as *all* the trade, but that it is 'something considerably more than merely some of the trade'. Regarding the requirement on external trade, the Appellate Body noted that it is not required that each constituent member of a customs union applies the *same* duties and other regulations of commerce as other constituent members with respect to trade with third countries, but only that 'substantially the same' duties and other regulations be applied, which offers a certain degree of flexibility to the constituent members of a customs union in 'the creation of a common commercial policy'. However, the Appellate Body cautioned that this 'flexibility' is limited. Something closely approaching 'sameness' is certainly required.

The specific requirements to be met by customs unions and free-trade areas can be found in paragraphs 5 and 8 of Article XXIV of the GATT 1994 and in the WTO Understanding on the Interpretation of Article XXIV. These WTO provisions also provide for the possibility of the formation of an 'interim agreement', or an agreement leading, within a certain period, to the establishment of a customs union or a free-trade area. The proposed period for the formation of the customs union or free-trade area, however, must be 'a reasonable length of time'. According to the Understanding on the Interpretation of Article XXIV, this reasonable length of time should not exceed ten years.

Significantly less demanding requirements for regional trade agreements between developing-country Members are provided in the Decision of the GATT Contracting Parties of 28 November 1979 on Differential and More Favourable Treatment, Reciprocity and Fuller Participation of Developing Countries (known as the Enabling Clause) (see Section 4.8).

4.7.2 Regional trade agreements on trade in services

For regional trade agreements on trade in services, referred to in the GATS as 'economic integration agreements', Article V of the GATS has similar requirements to Article XXIV of the GATT 1994. According to paragraphs 1 and 4 of this provision, a measure otherwise GATS-inconsistent, and in particular inconsistent with the MFN treatment obligation of the Article II of the GATS, is justified if:

- the measure is introduced as part of an agreement liberalizing trade in services that meets all the requirements set out in Article V (i.e. the requirement that the agreement must (1) have substantial sectoral coverage, (2) provide for the absence or elimination of substantially all discrimination between or among the parties in the covered sectors and (3) not raise the overall level of barriers to trade in services in the covered sectors for third countries); and
- WTO Members would be prevented from entering into such an agreement liberalizing trade in services if the measure concerned were not allowed.

With regard to economic integration agreements to which developing countries are parties, Article V:3(a) of the

GATS provides for flexibility regarding the conditions set out in Article V:1.

4.7.3 Review of conformity with the exceptions on regional trade agreements

It is often stated that, in practice, many regional trade agreements do not comply with the requirements of Article XXIV of the GATT 1994 and Article V of the GATS. WTO Members must notify the WTO of any regional trade agreement they conclude, and the WTO Committee on Regional Trade Agreements or the Committee on Trade and Development (for regional trade agreements between developing-country Members) review every notified agreement for WTO consistency. However, due to the consensus requirement (see Section 7.6), these Committees have, since 1995, never come to a decision concerning the WTO conformity of a regional trade agreement.

The conformity of regional trade agreements with the exceptions in Article XXIV of the GATT, Article V of the GATS or the Enabling Clause can be challenged through the WTO dispute settlement mechanism. However, WTO Members have, to date, been very hesitant to have recourse to WTO dispute settlement regarding the WTO consistency of a regional trade agreement. In view of the fact that all WTO Members (except for Mongolia) are part of one or more regional trade agreement(s), the WTO consistency of which may be challenged, this is probably not surprising.

In the context of the Doha Round negotiations, Members have reached agreement on a Transparency

Mechanism for Regional Trade Agreements, improving on the existing transparency obligations and enabling Members to have more detailed information on proposed and new regional trade agreements and to facilitate their consideration in the relevant Committees.

4.8 Exceptions for economic development

Finally, WTO law provides for exceptions for economic development in favour of developing countries. Almost all WTO agreements provide for special and differential treatment provisions for developing-country Members to facilitate their integration into the world trading system and to promote their economic development. These provisions, also referred to as 'S&D treatment' provisions, can be divided into six categories:

- provisions aimed at increasing the trade opportunities of developing-country Members;
- provisions under which WTO Members should safeguard the interests of developing country Members;
- flexibility of commitments, of action, and use of policy instruments;
- transitional time periods;
- technical assistance; and
- provisions relating to least-developed-country Members.

Some examples of S&D treatment provisions were mentioned earlier (Sections 4.5.3.1, 4.6, 4.7.1 and 4.7.2). Other examples of S&D treatment provisions are (1) a developing-country Member has the right to temporarily impose higher import duties than its tariff bindings to promote the establishment of a new industry (known as the 'infant industry' exception in Article XVIII:A of the GATT 1994); (2) safeguard measures may not be applied against imports from a developing-country Member if its share of imports of the product concerned in the importing Member does not exceed 3 per cent (Article 9 of the Agreement on Safeguards); (3) special regard must be given by developed-country Members to the specific situation of developing-country Members when considering the application of anti-dumping measures (Article 15 of the Anti-Dumping Agreement, see Section 5.2.6); (4) some developing countries have been exempted from the prohibition on export subsidies (Article 27 of the SCM Agreement, see Section 5.3.6); (5) the special needs of developing-country Members must be taken into account by other Members when preparing and applying sanitary and phytosanitary measures (Article 10.1 of the SPS Agreement, see Section 6.3.2) and technical regulations, standards and conformity assessment procedures (Article 12.3 of the TBT Agreement, see Section 6.2.2; and (6) longer transitional periods have been granted to least-developed country Members to implement their obligations under the TRIPS Agreement (Article 66.1 of the TRIPS Agreement, see Section 6.4.2).

The Enabling Clause mentioned earlier (see Section 4.7.1), which is now part of the GATT 1994, allows developed-country Members to grant preferential tariff treatment to imports from developing countries. This exception thus allows Members to deviate from the basic MFN treatment obligation of Article I:1 of the GATT 1994 in order to promote the economic development of developing-country

Members. Examples of the arrangements allowed under the Enabling Clause are:

- the Generalized System of Preferences (GSP) schemes of, *inter alia*, the European Union, the United States, Japan and Australia under which they grant preferential tariff treatment to developing countries under certain conditions; and
- the Everything But Arms arrangement, under which the European Union does not impose import duties or quotas on products of least-developed countries.

A WTO Member can, under the Enabling Clause, grant additional preferential tariff treatment to some developing countries and not to others, on the condition that the WTO Member involved treats all 'similarly situated' developing-country Members equally. Similarly situated developing-country Members are all those that have the development, financial and trade needs to which the additional preferential tariff treatment is intended to respond. The determination of whether developing-country Members are similarly situated must be based on objective criteria.

In *EC – Tariff Preferences (2004)*, the Generalized System of Preferences of the European Communities was at issue. It provided, in addition to its general tariff preferences for all developing countries and its additional tariff preferences for least-developed countries, certain 'special incentive arrangements' in the form of additional tariff preferences linked to the protection of labour rights, the protection of the environment and the fight against

138

drug production and trafficking. The tariff preferences under latter of these arrangements (known as the Drug Arrangements) were granted to twelve specific countries only (including Pakistan). India challenged these additional preferences as inconsistent with the non-discrimination requirement of the Enabling Clause. The Appellate Body found that because the Drug Arrangements provided for a closed list of twelve identified beneficiaries and contained no criteria or standards to provide a basis for distinguishing developing-country Members that are beneficiaries under the Drug Arrangements from other developing-country Members, they did not provide identical treatment to 'similarly situated' developing-country Members and thus could not be justified under the Enabling Clause.

Further reading
General and security exceptions

Andersen, H. (2015) 'Protection of non-trade values in WTO Appellate Body jurisprudence: exceptions, economic arguments, and eluding questions', *Journal of International Economic Law* 18 383–405.

Bronckers, M., and Maskus, E. K. (2014) 'China–Raw Materials: a controversial step towards evenhanded exploitation of natural resources', *World Trade Review* 13 393–408.

Howse, R., and Langille, J. (2012) 'Permitting pluralism: the Seal Products dispute and why the WTO should accept trade restrictions justified by noninstrumental moral values', *Yale Journal of International Law* 37 367–432.

Kapterian, G. (2010) 'A critique of the WTO jurisprudence on 'necessity', *International and Comparative Law Quarterly* 59(1) 89–127.

Pickett, E., and Lux, M. (2015) 'Embargo as a trade defense against an embargo: the WTO compatibility of the Russian ban on imports from the EU', *Global Trade and Customs Journal* 10(1) 2–41.

Exceptions for safeguard measures

Bown, P.C., and Wu, M. (2014) 'Safeguards and the perils of preferential trade agreements: Dominican Republic–Safeguard Measures', *World Trade Review* 13 179–227.

Rodríguez, M. P. (2007) 'Safeguards in the World Trade Organization ten years after: a dissociated state of the law'? *Journal of World Trade* 41(1) 159–190.

Exceptions for regional trade agreements

Altemöller, F. (2015) 'A future for multilateralism?: new regionalism, counter-multilateralism and perspectives for the world trade system after the Bali Ministerial Conference', *Global Trade and Customs Journal* 10(1) 42–53.

Brink, T. (2010) 'Which WTO Rules can a PTA lawfully breach? Completing the analysis in Brazil – Tyres', *Journal of World Trade* 44(4) 813–846.

Exceptions for economic development

Charnovitz, S., Bartels, L., Howse, R., Bradley, J., Pauwelyn, J., and Regan, D. (2004) 'The Appellate Body's GSP decision', *World Trade Review* 3 239–265.

Chapter 5

Rules on unfair trade

5.1 Introduction

WTO law provides for detailed rules with respect to dumping and subsidization – two specific trade practices commonly considered to be unfair. The following sections will briefly examine the WTO rules concerning these unfair trade practices.

5.2 Rules on dumping

The WTO rules on dumping are contained in Article VI of the GATT 1994 and in the Anti-Dumping Agreement.

'Dumping' is defined in Article 2.1 of the Anti-Dumping Agreement as bringing a product onto the market of another country at a price less than the 'normal value' of that product.

WTO law does not prohibit dumping. Since prices of products are usually set by private companies, not by governments, WTO law does not regulate dumping itself. Instead, it governs the actions of WTO Members in response to dumping. WTO Members are allowed to take measures to protect their domestic industry from the injurious effects of dumping. Pursuant to Article VI of the GATT 1994 and the Anti-Dumping Agreement, WTO Members are entitled to impose anti-dumping measures if three substantive conditions are met:

- there is dumping;
- the domestic industry producing the like product in the importing country is suffering material injury (or there is a threat of such material injury); and
- there is a causal link between the dumping and the injury.

These requirements have been worked out in detail in Articles 2 to 4 of the Anti-Dumping Agreement. The Anti-Dumping Agreement further provides rules concerning anti-dumping investigations and the imposition and collection of anti-dumping duties.

WTO Members have frequent recourse to anti-dumping measures, and these measures are regularly the subject of trade disputes between WTO Members.

> More than three thousand anti-dumping measures have been imposed by WTO Members since the establishment of the WTO. Between 1 January 1995 and 31 December 2014, the most frequent user of anti-dumping measures was India (534 measures), followed at a distance by the United States (345 measures), the European Union (298 measures) and Argentina (228 measures). This makes clear that the days when anti-dumping measures were almost exclusively used by developed-country Members are over. China has been by far the biggest target of anti-dumping measures (759 measures), followed by Korea (213 measures), Chinese Taipei (173 measures) and the United States (162 measures). To date, 112 disputes have been brought claiming violations of Article VI of the GATT 1994 and/or the Anti-Dumping Agreement.

5.2.1 *Dumping*

A product is considered to be 'dumped' if its export price is less than the 'normal value' of that product. In order to determine whether dumping has taken place, generally a price-to-price comparison of the 'normal value' with the 'export price' of the product must be conducted. The difference between these two prices is the margin of dumping. This margin is important because the anti-dumping duty applied may not exceed this margin.

The 'normal value' of a product, according to Article 2.1 of the Anti-Dumping Agreement, is the comparable price in the ordinary course of trade of the like product in the domestic market of the exporter or producer. For domestic sales transactions to be used in the determination of the normal value of a product:

- the sale must be in the ordinary course of trade;
- the sale must be of the 'like product';
- the product must be destined for consumption in the exporting country; and
- the prices of the products at issue must be comparable.

Factors that *may* lead to the determination that sales are not 'in the ordinary course of trade' are the fact that the sales are between affiliated parties or the fact that products are sold below production costs or are sold at abnormally high or low prices. Sales transactions conducted under such circumstances must be disregarded in the determination of the 'normal value' of the product.

Unlike the GATT 1994, the Anti-Dumping Agreement does provide for a definition of 'like products' in Article 2.6. A 'like product' is defined as a product that is identical (i.e. alike in all respects) or, in the absence of such a product, a product which has characteristics closely resembling those of the product under consideration.

In order to ensure that the prices of products are 'comparable', Article 2.4 of the Anti-Dumping Agreement requires that due allowance (i.e. adjustments) be made for factors that affect price comparability, such as the level of trade of the products (usually the ex-factory level), the timing of the sale, differences in physical characteristics, terms of sale and taxation.

In certain circumstances, the domestic price of the like product on the market of the exporting country does not produce an appropriate 'normal value'. This is the case when sales in the market of the exporting country are made below cost or when, because of the particular market situation or because there are no, or too few, sales of the like product 'in the ordinary course of trade' in the market of the exporting country, a proper comparison with the export price is not possible. In such cases, Article 2.2 of the Anti-Dumping Agreement provides that the normal value can be determined by one of two alternative methods:

- using a 'representative' export price to an appropriate third country as the normal value; or
- constructing the normal value on the basis of production costs plus a reasonable amount for administrative, selling and general costs and for profit.

144

Where the exporting country is a non-market economy (NME), that is, an economy where the government has a (substantially) complete monopoly of its trade and where all domestic prices are fixed by the State, the domestic price of the like product obviously does not produce an appropriate 'normal value'. In the particular situation where the exporting country is an NME, and the market situation is therefore 'particular', importing countries exercise significant discretion in the calculation of normal value. They have, for example, determined the normal value on the basis the price of the like product on the domestic market of an appropriate third country (the analogue country method).

Because the prices of fasteners on the market of the exporting country, China, were considered to be distorted and could therefore not be used to the determine the normal value, in the dumping investigation at issue in *EC – Fasteners (China) (2011)*, the European Commission determined the normal value of the fasteners of the Chinese exporters on the basis of the prices of fasteners produced and sold in India, the analogue country chosen by the European Union.

Once the normal value of the product has been determined, it must be compared to the export price in order to determine the existence and extent of dumping. The export price of the product is ordinarily based on the transaction price at which the producer in the exporting country sells the product to an importer in the importing country. The Anti-Dumping Agreement provides for an alternative where this method of export price determination is not appropriate, for example, if an association between the producer/exporter and the importer affects the transaction price. In this case, Article 2.3 of the Anti-Dumping Agreement permits a WTO Member to construct the export price based on the price at which the product is first sold to an independent buyer or, if this is not possible, on another 'reasonable' basis.

The normal value and export price are subsequently compared to establish the margin of dumping. This comparison should normally be done transaction-to-transaction or weighted-average-to-weighted-average. However, in particular circumstances, a comparison of the weighted average normal value to export prices in individual transactions is allowed. As stated earlier, according to Article 2.4 of the Anti-Dumping Agreement, the comparison must be fair, and due allowance must be made for factors affecting price comparability. The question of the adjustments necessary to ensure a fair comparison between the normal value and the export price is often one of the most contentious aspects of an anti-dumping investigation.

Margins of dumping can be positive or negative: they are positive when the export price is lower than the normal value (in which case dumping exists) and negative when the export price is higher than the normal value (in which case no dumping exists). Some WTO Members treated negative dumping margins found with regard to some transactions or groups of transactions as zero (a practice known as 'zeroing') and considered in the calculation of the overall dumping margin only the positive dumping margins found with regard to other transactions or groups of transactions. It is clear that 'zeroing' artificially inflates the magnitude of dumping, resulting in the determination of a larger overall dumping margin, and thus permitting the imposition of a higher anti-dumping duty. The 'zeroing' practice was at issue in a number of disputes (such as *EC – Bed Linen (2001), US – Zeroing (EC) (2006), US – Zeroing (Japan) (2007)* and *US – Stainless Steel (Mexico)(2008)*). The Appellate Body has repeatedly concluded that this 'zeroing' practice (and its variants) is inconsistent with the 'fair comparison' requirement of Article 2.4 of the Anti-Dumping Agreement.

5.2.2 *Material injury or the threat thereof*

The second condition for the imposition of an anti-dumping duty is that the domestic industry producing the like product in the importing country is suffering material injury or is under threat thereof.

Article 4.1 of the Anti-Dumping Agreement defines the 'domestic industry' generally as 'the domestic producers as a whole of the like products or … those of them whose collective output of the products constitutes a major proportion of the total domestic production of those products'. According to well-established case law, a 'major proportion of the total domestic production' is not the same as the 'majority' of the production; 40 per cent of the production could be a major proportion, depending on the specific circumstances of the case.

In *EC – Fasteners (China) (2011)*, the Appellate Body noted that Article 4.1 of the Anti-Dumping Agreement does not specify a particular proportion for evaluating whether certain producers constitute 'a major proportion of the domestic industry' but held that the context of the term indicates that it should be understood to mean 'a relatively high proportion of the domestic production'. The Appellate Body stressed the need to minimize the risk of distortion of the injury assessment that may arise from the exclusion of some producers from the 'domestic industry'. Thus, 'a major proportion' of domestic production must be determined so as to ensure that the domestic industry defined in this way is capable of providing ample data that ensure an accurate injury analysis.

Injury is defined in footnote 9 to Article 3 of the Anti-Dumping Agreement to mean one of three things:

- *material* injury to the domestic industry (a lower threshold of injury than *serious* injury required for safeguard measures, see Section 4.5.1.2);
- threat of material injury to the domestic industry; or
- material retardation of the establishment of a domestic industry.

The determination of injury, according to Article 3.1 of the Anti-Dumping Agreement, must be based on positive evidence and involve an objective examination of both (1) the volume of the dumped imports and the effect of the dumped imports on the domestic market price for 'like products' and (2) the consequent impact of these imports on the domestic producers of such products. Article 3.2 elaborates how the investigating authority is to consider whether there has been a significant increase in the volume of dumped imports and what the effect of the dumped imports has been on the price of the like domestic products (significant price undercutting, price depression and/or price suppression). Article 3.4 sets out a list of economic factors having a bearing on the state of the domestic industry that must be examined and considered in the injury determination: sales volumes, profits, output, market share, productivity, return on investments, utilization of the production capacity of the domestic industry, factors affecting domestic prices, the magnitude of the margin of dumping, and negative effects on cash flow, inventories, employment, wages, growth, ability to raise capital or investments. This list of factors is not exhaustive, but consideration of the factors listed is a mandatory minimum.

A determination of a threat of material injury must be based on facts and not merely on allegation, conjecture or remote possibility (Article 3.7 of the Anti-Dumping Agreement). A threat of material injury exists when a change in circumstances, creating a situation where dumping would cause injury, is imminent and foreseen.

A determination of 'material retardation' of the establishment of a domestic industry must be based on convincing evidence that such an industry is actually forthcoming (e.g. the existence of advanced plans for a new industry, a factory under construction or new capital equipment already having been ordered).

149

5.2.3 *Causal link*

The third and final requirement for the imposition of anti-dumping duties is the demonstration of a causal link between the dumped imports and the injury to the domestic industry, as required by Article 3.5 of the Anti-Dumping Agreement. The dumping must be a genuine and substantial cause of material injury to the domestic industry but does not need to be the sole or the principal cause of this injury. The investigating authority must examine other known factors that are contributing to the injury, and the part of the injury that is caused by other factors may not be attributed to the dumped imports (known as the 'non-attribution' requirement). Article 3.5 provides an illustrative list of other possible factors that may cause injury.

Industria's smartphone industry has seen its profits sharply decrease and its market share halved in the past ten months. During this period the investigating authority of Industria has established the existence of increased volumes of dumped smartphones exported by certain Agricolan smartphone producers. However, in this same period, the Industrian smartphone industry has been subject to strong competition from more technologically advanced smartphones originating in Alpinia, which Industrian consumers seem to prefer. In addition, new Industrian legislation imposing recycling requirements on domestic producers of electronic products has led to increased costs for Industrian smartphone producers. In establishing whether the dumped smartphone imports from Agricola are a genuine and substantial cause of the injury being suffered by Industrian smartphone producers, the Industrian investigating authority must examine the other injury-causing factors and must separate and distinguish their injurious effects from those of the dumped imports in order to ensure that this part of the injury is not attributed to the dumped imports.

5.2.4 Anti-dumping investigations

The Anti-Dumping Agreement also sets out in considerable detail rules according to which the investigating authorities of a Member must initiate and conduct an anti-dumping investigation. According to Article 1 of the Anti-Dumping Agreement, anti-dumping measures may only be applied pursuant to investigations that are consistent with these detailed rules. Such consistency is often at issue in disputes regarding anti-dumping measures.

Articles 5 and 6 of the Anti-Dumping Agreement set out the requirements that govern national anti-dumping investigations and the evidentiary rules that apply in these investigations. Furthermore, notification and publication obligations that must be complied with by the competent authority are provided in Article 12 of the Anti-Dumping Agreement. Finally, Article 13 of the Anti-Dumping Agreement requires the existence of independent judicial, arbitral or administrative tribunals or procedures for review of final determinations or reviews of determinations in anti-dumping procedures.

The main objectives of all these procedural rules are to ensure that:

- the investigations are conducted in an objective and transparent manner;
- all interested parties have the opportunity to defend their interests; and
- the investigating authorities adequately explain the basis for their determinations.

5.2.5 *Imposition of anti-dumping measures*

If, following an anti-dumping investigation, a final determination of the existence of dumping, injury and causation has been made, a Member may, but is not obliged to, impose definitive anti-dumping duties. Articles 9 to 11 of the Anti-Dumping Agreement regulate the imposition and collection of anti-dumping duties. Note that an anti-dumping duty:

- may never exceed the margin of dumping (i.e. the difference between the normal value and the export price of the product at issue);
- may only be applied as long as and to the extent necessary to counteract injurious dumping (determined through periodic review at the initiative of the investigating authority or upon request by an interested party); and
- must be terminated at the latest five years after having been imposed, unless it is established in a review before that date ('sunset review') that this would be likely to lead to a continuation or recurrence of dumping *and* injury.

Note that Members are encouraged to impose anti-dumping duties that are less than the margin of dumping if such lesser duties would be adequate to remove the injury to the domestic industry (commonly known as the 'lesser duty rule').

Anti-dumping duties must be collected on a non-discriminatory basis – in other words, they are imposed on all imports, regardless of their origin, that are found to be dumped and causing injury. When anti-dumping duties are imposed, the investigating authorities must, in principle, calculate a dumping margin for each known exporter/producer individually. However, in practice, when the number of exporters/producers is so large as to make individual calculations impracticable, Article 6.10 of the Anti-Dumping Agreement allows the investigating authorities to use 'sampling', that is, to limit the number of exporters/producers investigated individually and apply to all other exporters/producers the weighted average of the dumping margin established for individually investigated exporters/producers (i.e. the 'all others' rate).

Note that, aside from the possibility to apply definitive anti-dumping duties following a *final* finding of dumping, injury and causation, Article VI:2 of the GATT provides for two other permissible responses to dumping following a *preliminary* affirmative finding of dumping, injury and causation:

- provisional anti-dumping measures (that can be adopted during the investigation by the competent authority if necessary to prevent injury during this period); or

- voluntary price undertakings (where exporters agree to revise their export prices or cease exports at dumped prices in order to avoid the imposition of anti-dumping duties).

Detailed rules on the latter two measures are set out in Articles 7 and 8 of the Anti-Dumping Agreement. Aside from the three permissible responses mentioned in the Anti-Dumping Agreement, any other specific action against dumping is prohibited.

In *US – 1916 Act (2000)* the Appellate Body held that US legislation providing for civil and criminal proceedings and penalties against dumping violated Article VI:2 of the Anti-Dumping Agreement because these measures are not among the three permissible responses set out in this provision. Similarly, in *US – Offset Act (Byrd Amendment) (2003)*, the Appellate Body found a US law providing for the distribution of collected anti-dumping duties to the affected domestic industries to be in violation of Article 18.1 of the Anti-Dumping Agreement because these offset payments are not among the permissible responses to dumping.

5.2.6 Special and differential treatment for developing-country Members

Article 15 of the Anti-Dumping Agreement requires, in its first sentence, that developed-country Members give 'special regard' to the situation of developing-country Members when considering the application of anti-dumping measures. The second sentence of this Article provides 'operational indications' of the nature of the specific action required. It provides that, where the essential interests of developing countries would be affected, before applying anti-dumping duties, developed-country Members must explore 'the possibilities of constructive remedies' provided in the Anti-Dumping Agreement. These 'constructive remedies' have been held to include the imposition of a 'lesser duty' or a price undertaking (see Section 5.2.5). However, the nature of the obligation to *explore* 'the possibilities of constructive remedies' does not entail a duty to actually apply or accept a constructive remedy that may be identified or offered.

As held by the panel in *EC – Bed Linen (2001)*, 'the concept of *explore* clearly does not imply any particular outcome'. The panel recognized that exploration could lead to the conclusion that no constructive remedies are possible. However, it held that Article 15 of the Anti-Dumping Agreement does impose an obligation to actively consider with an open mind the possibility of a constructive remedy.

5.2.7 Standard of review

As noted earlier, consistency with the provisions of the Anti-Dumping Agreement has been challenged in a significant number of disputes. These disputes are subject to the general rules on WTO dispute settlement contained in the Dispute

Settlement Understanding (DSU) (see Chapter 8), *except as otherwise provided* in the Anti-Dumping Agreement. Article 17 of the Anti-Dumping Agreement contains special rules for dispute settlement, the most important of which are those on the standard of review to be applied by panels hearing disputes on anti-dumping measures.

As discussed in Section 8.6.2, Article 11 of the DSU sets out the standard of review for panels, providing that a panel must conduct 'an objective assessment of the matter before it, including an objective assessment of the facts of the case and the applicability of and conformity with the relevant covered agreements'. Article 17.6 of the Anti-Dumping Agreement, however, contains two special rules in this regard.

First, Article 17.6(i) provides that, in assessing the facts of the matter, the panel must establish whether the investigating authority's establishment of the facts was 'proper' and its evaluation of the facts was 'unbiased and objective'. If this is the case, the panel may not overturn the authority's evaluation even if the panel would have reached a different conclusion itself.

As held by the Appellate Body in *US – Hot-Rolled Steel (2001)*, the different roles of panels and the investigating authorities must be borne in mind. Investigating authorities are charged with the task of making the factual determinations relevant to their overall determinations of dumping and injury, whereas 'the task of panels is simply to review the investigating authorities' "establishment" and "evaluation" of the facts'.

Thus, the panel may not engage in a new and independent fact-finding exercise. Instead, its mandate is limited to assessing whether the investigating authority's evaluation was 'unbiased and objective'. In doing so, the panel must conduct an *objective* review of the investigating authority's establishment and evaluation of the facts. There is therefore no conflict between the standard of review under Article 11 of the DSU and Article 17.6(i) of the Anti-Dumping Agreement.

The second special rule is contained in Article 17.6(ii) of the Anti-Dumping Agreement. After reiterating the general rule contained in Article 3.2 of the DSU that the provisions of the Agreement must be interpreted in accordance with the customary rules on interpretation of public international law (see Section 8.2), it provides that, in the case of more than one permissible interpretation, the panel must find the authority's measure in conformity with the Anti-Dumping Agreement if it rests upon one of the permissible interpretations.

As held by the Appellate Body in *US – Continued Zeroing (2009)*, this provision allows for the possibility that the customary rules on treaty interpretation, codified in Articles 31 and 32 of the Vienna Convention on the Law of Treaties (VCLT), 'may give rise to an interpretative range'. In such a case, 'an interpretation falling within that range is permissible and must be given effect by holding the measure to be in conformity with [the Anti-Dumping Agreement]'. However, the rules of the VCLT aim at coherence and harmony and cannot give rise to interpretations with mutually *contradictory* results.

5.3 Rules on subsidization

The WTO rules on subsidies are found in the GATT 1994 and the Agreement on Subsidies and Countervailing Measures (SCM Agreement). The WTO treatment of subsidies differs from that of dumping. As discussed in Section 5.2, WTO law does not prohibit dumping. However, WTO law does prohibit certain categories of subsidies, and others may be challenged as WTO-inconsistent if they cause adverse effects to the interests of other Members. In addition, WTO law includes rules on countervailing measures (measures taken by Members in response to injurious subsidization). A distinction must thus be made between:

- rules concerning the subsidies themselves (see Article XVI of the GATT 1994 and Articles 3 to 9 of the SCM Agreement); and
- rules governing the imposition by Members of countervailing duties to protect their domestic industries from injury caused by the importation of subsidized products (see Article VI of the GATT 1994 and Articles 10 to 23 of the SCM Agreement).

Subsidies are a frequently used instrument of economic and social policy and may be used by Members to promote legitimate objectives. However, they may also have adverse effects on the interests of other Members whose industry may suffer from unfair competition from the subsidized products on its domestic or export markets.

Members have an obligation to notify (i.e. to report) their subsidies to the WTO. Examples of such notifications are the European Union's notification of the European Fisheries Fund, which provides support, *inter alia*, for the sustainable development of fisheries areas; Brazil's notification of PROFARMA, a support programme to encourage innovation in Brazil's pharmaceutical and medical devices industries; and the US notification of the Industrial Technologies Programme, providing support aimed at reducing the energy intensity of the US industrial sector. Disputes about subsidies have been prominent in WTO dispute settlement. There have been sixty-four such disputes, the most noteworthy of which were *EC and Certain Member States – Large Civil Aircraft (2011)* and *US – Large Civil Aircraft (2nd complaint) (2012)*, involving billions of euros and US dollars in subsidies to Airbus and Boeing, respectively.

Members have notified the imposition of 202 countervailing duties between 1 January 1995 and 31 December 2014. The biggest user of countervailing measures in this period has been the United States (86 measures), followed by the European Union (35 measures) and Canada (24 measures). The most frequent target of countervailing duties has been China (56 measures), followed by India (36 measures) and the European Union (12 measures). To date, the imposition of countervailing measures has been challenged in forty-five disputes.

5.3.1 *Subsidies covered by the SCM Agreement*

The definition of a 'subsidy' in Article 1.1 of the SCM Agreement comprises two elements. A 'subsidy' exists if:

- there is a financial contribution by a government or public body, or income or price support; and
- a benefit is conferred thereby.

It appears from this definition that for a financial contribution to qualify as a 'subsidy' for purposes of the SCM Agreement, it must be provided by a 'government or public body'. The term 'government' includes local and regional governments. The term 'public body' does not cover all entities owned and/or controlled by the government, but only those that possess, exercise or are vested with governmental authority.

Article 1.1 provides an exhaustive but broad list of types of 'financial contribution'. These are:

- direct transfers of funds (such as grants, loans and equity infusions) or potential direct transfers of funds or liabilities (such as loan guarantees);
- government revenue, otherwise due, that is foregone or not collected (such as tax exemptions);
- the provision by a government of goods or services other than general infrastructure, or the purchase by a government of goods; and
- government payments to a funding mechanism, or financial contributions through a private body (the latter category of financial contributions covers situations where a government entrusts or directs a private body to effectuate

one of the first three types of financial contributions and operates to prevent circumvention of the disciplines on subsidies).

As stated earlier, income or price support that confers a benefit also is covered by the definition of a subsidy. This category does not cover all government interventions that may have an effect on prices but only direct government intervention in the market with the aim to fix the price of a good at a particular level.

To qualify as a 'subsidy', the financial contribution or income or price support must confer a 'benefit' to the recipient. Whether there has been a cost to the government is irrelevant in this context. A benefit to the recipient exists if the recipient is 'better off' than it would have been without the financial contribution. Article 14 of the SCM Agreement sets out guidelines for the calculation of the amount of subsidy in terms of the 'benefit to the recipient'. According to these guidelines, a 'benefit to the recipient' exists if the financial contribution was received on terms *more favourable* than those available to the recipient in the market.

Agricola puts into place an economic stimulus package for its chocolate industry comprising government loans to chocolate producers at lower than commercial interest rates, government provision of cocoa powder to the chocolate industry at lower than market prices, access for chocolate producers to free laboratory services for cadmium testing of chocolate, and government purchase of chocolate for children's hospitals at higher than market prices. All these stimulus measures are financial contributions conferring a benefit to the chocolate industry and therefore subsidies within the meaning of Article 1.1 of the SCM Agreement.

Furthermore, Article 1.2 of the SCM Agreement provides that this Agreement only applies to 'specific' subsidies, as opposed to subsidies that are widely available within an economy. The latter subsidies are presumed not to distort the allocation of resources within that economy and, therefore, are not subject to the disciplines of the SCM Agreement. Article 2.1 of the SCM Agreement sets out three principles for determining whether a subsidy is 'specific'. First, subparagraph (a) of Article 2.1 establishes that a subsidy is specific if the granting authority, or the legislation pursuant to which the granting authority operates, *explicitly* limits access to that subsidy to certain enterprises or industries. Second, subparagraph (b) of Article 2.1 of the SCM Agreement stipulates that a subsidy shall not be considered 'specific' if the granting authority, or the legislation pursuant to which the granting authority operates, establishes *objective* criteria or conditions governing the eligibility for, and the amount of, the subsidy, provided that (1) eligibility is automatic, (2) such criteria or conditions are strictly adhered to, and (3) the criteria or conditions are clearly spelled out in an official document so as to be capable of verification. Third, subparagraph (c) of Article 2.1 of the SCM Agreement establishes that, 'notwithstanding any appearance of non-specificity' resulting from the application of Article 2.1(a) and (b), a subsidy may nevertheless be found to be de facto specific on the basis of the consideration of 'other factors'. These factors are listed in Article 2.1(c), namely: (1) the use of a subsidy programme by a limited number of certain enterprises, (2) the predominant use of a subsidy programme by certain enterprises, (3) the granting of disproportionately large subsidies to certain enterprises, and (4) the manner in which discretion has been exercised by the granting authority in the decision to grant a subsidy.

In addition to the principles for determining specificity set out in Article 2.1, Article 2, in paragraph 2, establishes that subsidies which are limited to certain enterprises in a designated geographical region within the jurisdiction of the granting authority are specific and, in paragraph 3, establishes that all prohibited subsidies (i.e. export subsidies and import substitution subsidies) (see Section 5.3.2) shall be deemed to be specific.

Note that the focus of the specificity analysis is not on whether the financial contribution or income/price support has been *granted* to specific enterprises or industries but rather on whether *eligibility* to receive the financial contribution or income/price support is limited to specific enterprises or industries.

> In an effort to increase the competitiveness of its smartphone industry, Industria provides interest-free loans, for which only smartphone producers are eligible. Furthermore, Industria grants a reduction in company taxes to any firms that export more than 25 per cent of their total production. In addition, Industria controls

> energy prices in its territory to ensure the provision of low-cost electricity to all firms on its territory that meet the criteria for 'small and medium-sized enterprises' as set out in the relevant regulation. The first two of these measures meet the 'specificity' requirement for 'subsidies' within the meaning of Article 1.1 of the SCM Agreement. However, the third measure does not and is thus not a 'subsidy' for purposes of the SCM Agreement.

5.3.2 Prohibited subsidies

As noted earlier, the SCM Agreement distinguishes between those subsidies that are prohibited and those that are actionable (i.e. can be challenged) if they cause adverse effects to the interests of another WTO Member. Article 3 of the SCM Agreement explicitly prohibits:

- export subsidies, meaning subsidies that are contingent upon export performance; (see the illustrative list in Annex I to the SCM Agreement); and
- import substitution subsidies, meaning subsidies that are contingent upon the use of domestic over imported products.

A subsidy is 'contingent' on export performance or on import substitution if the grant of the subsidy is 'conditional or dependent' on export performance or import substitution. The mere fact that a subsidy is granted to an export-oriented firm is not sufficient to qualify this subsidy as an export contingent subsidy. Contingency on export or on import substitution may be either de jure (expressly stated or implicit in the words used in the measure) or de facto (in fact tied to anticipated exportation/export earnings or import substitution). The standard for the determination of de facto contingency is not a subjective one based on the intention of the government granting the subsidy, but rather an objective one based on the 'total configuration of facts constituting and surrounding the granting of the subsidy'.

As stated by the Appellate Body in *EC and Certain Member States – Large Civil Aircraft (2011)*, de facto export contingency is present when 'the granting of the subsidy is geared to induce the promotion of future export performance of the recipient'.

Subsidies contingent on exportation or on import substitution are commonly known as 'red light' subsidies and are prohibited because they aim to affect trade and are most likely to cause adverse effects to other Members.

When a dispute on prohibited subsidies arises, Article 4 of the SCM Agreement provides for timeframes that are only half the normal timeframes for dispute settlement proceedings (see Section 8.7.1). If a panel finds a measure to be a prohibited subsidy within the meaning of Article 3 of the SCM Agreement, it must recommend that the subsidy be withdrawn (i.e. removed) by the WTO Member without delay, and it must specify the time period within which withdrawal must take place. If a recommendation for withdrawal is not complied with within the time period set by the panel, the DSB must, upon request by the complainant(s) and by reverse consensus, authorize 'appropriate countermeasures' against the subsidizing Member. Appropriate countermeasures differ from the 'suspension of concessions or other obligations' (i.e. retaliation measures) under the DSU (see Section 8.6.4) in that the level of appropriate countermeasures could be the amount of the subsidy rather than the level of nullification or impairment of benefits arising from the WTO-inconsistent measure.

5.3.3 *Actionable subsidies*

Unlike export subsidies and import substitution subsidies, most subsidies are not prohibited. However, in terms of Article 5 of the SCM Agreement, they are subject to challenge (i.e. actionable) in the event that they cause adverse effects to the interests of another Member.

Article 5 of the SCM Agreement identifies three types of 'adverse effects' to the interests of other Members:

- injury to the domestic industry of another Member (Article 5(a));
- nullification or impairment of benefits accruing directly or indirectly to other Members under the GATT 1994 (Article 5(b)); and
- serious prejudice, or threat thereof, to the interests of another Member (Article 5(c)).

The concept of 'injury' to the domestic industry, within the meaning of Article 5(a) of the SCM Agreement, covers material injury, or the threat thereof, to a domestic industry producing the like product. As in the Anti-Dumping Agreement, 'like product' is defined in footnote 46 of the SCM Agreement as a product that is identical or, in the absence of such a product, has characteristics closely resembling those of the product under consideration. The definitions of 'domestic industry', 'material injury' and 'threat of material injury', as well as the requirement to demonstrate a causal link between the subsidy and the injury are, *mutatis mutandis*, very similar to the definitions and the requirements of the Anti-Dumping Agreement discussed in Sections 5.2.2 and 5.2.3.

The nullification or impairment of benefits of a WTO Member, as provided in Article 5(b), concerns, above all, benefits arising from tariff concessions bound under Article II:1 of the GATT 1994 (see Section 3.2). It is clear that subsidies can undermine improved market access resulting from tariff concessions.

'Serious prejudice' to the interests of another Member, as provided in Article 5(c), may arise in the following situations according to Article 6.3 of the SCM Agreement:

- where a subsidy displaces or impedes the import of a like product of another Member into the market of the subsidizing Member;
- where the subsidy displaces or impedes the export of a like product of another Member into the market of a third country;
- where the subsidy results in a significant price undercutting by the subsidized product in comparison to the like product of another Member in the same market or in significant price suppression, price depression or lost sales; or

- where the subsidy leads to an increase in the world market share of the subsidizing WTO Member in a particular primary product or commodity.

In *EC and Certain Member States – Large Civil Aircraft (2011)*, the Appellate Body examined whether various subsidies granted by the European Union and certain EU Member States to Airbus resulted in 'serious prejudice' to the interests of the United States. The Appellate Body assessed, *inter alia*, whether subsidies in the form of launch aid granted to Airbus resulted in 'displacement' of the like product – similar models of Boeing from the United States – from the markets of certain third countries including Australia. It recalled that the panel had found that Airbus's market share in Australia increased by 18 per cent between 2001 and 2005, whereas Boeing's market share declined by the same amount. It thus found 'displacement' by Airbus of similar models of Boeing from the Australian market. The Appellate Body also examined whether serious prejudice in the form of 'lost sales' had occurred. 'Lost sales' are sales that suppliers of the complaining Member, in this case Boeing, failed to obtain and that instead were won by suppliers of the respondent Member, here Airbus. The Appellate Body agreed with the panel's finding that, in specific sales campaigns, Boeing had lost sales to Airbus involving purchases by airlines such as easyJet, Air Berlin, Czech Airlines and Qantas. Consequently, 'serious prejudice' was found to exist.

Article 7 of the SCM Agreement provides for dispute settlement procedures for actionable subsidies. These procedures provide shorter timeframes than the normal dispute settlement proceedings in the DSU (see Section 8.7.1) but not as short as those applicable in the case of prohibited subsidies. If a panel and/or the Appellate Body finds that the subsidy at issue causes adverse effects to the interests of another WTO Member, then the subsidizing WTO Member has a choice between:

- taking appropriate steps to remove the adverse effects of the subsidy; or
- withdrawing the subsidy.

This must occur within six months of the adoption of the panel and/or Appellate Body report by the DSB. If not, the DSB must authorize, at the request of the complainant(s) and by reverse consensus, commensurate countermeasures (i.e. measures commensurate with the degree and nature of the adverse effects determined to exist) against the subsidizing WTO Member.

5.3.4 Non-actionable subsidies

In addition to prohibited and actionable subsidies, the SCM Agreement refers to 'non-actionable subsidies'. Currently, this category of subsidies only includes non-specific subsidies, which, as discussed earlier, are not subject to the disciplines of the SCM Agreement. Until 31 December 1999, this category further included certain types of specific subsidies listed in Article 8.2 of the SCM Agreement. These are, under narrowly circumscribed conditions, development assistance to certain disadvantaged regions, assistance to promote adaptation of existing facilities to new environmental requirements and assistance for research activities. This 'safe harbour' lapsed and was not renewed by Members. Consequently, at present, these subsidies are actionable, provided that they are specific.

5.3.5 Countervailing measures

Prohibited subsidies or subsidies that cause adverse effects to the interests of other Members may be challenged under the *multilateral* procedures of Articles 4 and 7 of the SCM Agreement, as set out earlier. In the alternative, with respect to any specific subsidy that causes *injury* to the domestic industry of the importing Member, this Member may choose to *unilaterally* impose duties, known as 'countervailing duties', to offset the effect of such subsidies. Article VI of the GATT 1994 and Articles 10 and 32 of the SCM Agreement set out the requirements for WTO Members to impose countervailing duties; namely, that:

- there are subsidized imports (i.e. imports of products from producers who benefited, or benefit, from specific subsidies, within the meaning of Articles 1, 2 and 14 of the SCM Agreement);
- there is material injury, or the threat thereof, to the domestic industry producing 'like products', as provided in Articles 15 and 16 of the SCM Agreement; and
- there is a causal link between the subsidized imports and the injury to the domestic industry, and injury caused by

other factors is not attributed to the subsidized imports, as required by Article 15.5 of the SCM Agreement.

The SCM Agreement provides detailed rules regarding the determination of subsidization (in Articles 1, 2 and 14), of material injury, or threat thereof, to the domestic industry (in Articles 15 and 16) and of a causal link between them. These requirements are discussed in Sections 5.3.1 and 5.3.3 and apply, *mutatis mutandis*, to the imposition of countervailing duties.

Aside from meeting the substantive requirements for the imposition of countervailing measures, Members must comply with the procedural rules for the conduct of a countervailing investigation before imposing countervailing duties. Articles 11–13 and 22 of the SCM Agreement provide detailed procedural requirements regarding the initiation and conduct of a countervailing investigation by the competent authorities of a Member imposing countervailing duties on subsidized imports. These rules are largely similar to the previously discussed rules for anti-dumping investigations set out in the Anti-Dumping Agreement (Section 5.2.4).

Finally, Articles 19, 20 and 21 of the SCM Agreement regulate the imposition and collection of *definitive* countervailing duties upon a final determination of the existence of subsidized imports, injury and causation. In this regard, it is important to note that a final countervailing duty:

- may never exceed the amount of the subsidy (calculated in terms of subsidization per unit of the subsidized product);
- may only be applied as long as and to the extent necessary to counteract the injurious subsidy (determined through

periodic review at the initiative of the investigating authority or upon request by an interested party);
- must be terminated at the latest five years after having been imposed, unless it is established in a review before that date ('sunset review') that this would be likely to lead to a continuation or repetition of subsidization and injury.

If the amount of injury caused is less than the full amount of the subsidy, the definitive countervailing duty should preferably be limited to the amount necessary to counteract the injury caused (the 'lesser-duty rule'). According to Article 19.3 of the SCM Agreement, countervailing duties must be imposed in the 'appropriate amounts' in each case. This requirement has been interpreted as prohibiting the application of 'double remedies'; that is, offsetting the same subsidization twice by the concurrent imposition of anti-dumping duties and countervailing duties against the same imports. This situation may arise when anti-dumping duties are calculated in the basis of non-market economy methodology (see Section 5.2.1). According to Article 19.3 of the SCM Agreement, countervailing duties must also be imposed on a non-discriminatory basis on imports from all sources found to be subsidized and causing injury.

Note that Articles 17 and 18 of the SCM Agreement provide for two other permissible responses to injurious subsidization that may be used after a *preliminary* determination of subsidized imports, injury and causation:

- provisional countervailing measures (that can be adopted during the investigation by the competent authorities if necessary to prevent injury during this period); or

- voluntary undertakings in terms of which, in order to avoid the imposition of countervailing measures, (1) the subsidizing Member undertakes to eliminate or limit the subsidy or take other measures concerning its effects or (2) the exporter undertakes to revise its prices to eliminate the injurious effect of the subsidy.

According to Article 32.1 of the SCM Agreement, no specific action against the subsidy of another Member may be taken, aside from the four measures mentioned earlier: namely, voluntary undertakings, provisional countervailing measures, definitive countervailing duties and multilaterally sanctioned countermeasures taken following dispute settlement proceedings.

Note that, with regard to a particular subsidy, a Member may invoke in parallel the provisions of the SCM Agreement relating to the *multilateral* procedures regarding prohibited and actionable subsidies *and* the provisions regarding the *unilateral* imposition of countervailing duties. However, only *one* form of remedy (either a countervailing duty *or* a countermeasure) may be imposed with regard to a particular subsidy.

5.3.6 *Special and differential treatment of developing countries*

In recognition of the important role that subsidies can play in the economic development programmes of developing-country Members, Article 27 of the SCM Agreement provides more flexible rules for these Members. In particular,

Article 27.2 grants an exemption from the prohibition on export subsidies for least-developed country Members and developing-country Members with a gross national product below US$1000 per capita. Instead, the export subsidies of these Members are treated in the same way as 'actionable subsidies' and may be challenged according to the procedures set out in Article 7 of the SCM Agreement. In addition, Article 27.13 provides that certain subsidies that would normally be actionable are not actionable if granted by developing-country Members in the context of privatization programmes (e.g. direct forgiveness of debt and subsidies to cover social costs).

With regard to the imposition of countervailing duties against imports from developing-country Members, Article 27.10 sets certain *de minimis* thresholds below which such imports are not countervailable; namely where (1) the overall level of subsidies to the relevant product is not more than 2 per cent *ad valorem*, or (2) the volume of the subsidized imports is less than 4 per cent of the total imports of the like product of the importing Member, unless the collective share of imports from such Members exceeds 9 per cent of the total imports of like products.

5.3.7 *Agricultural subsidies*

The Agreement on Agriculture provides for special rules on agricultural export subsidies and domestic agricultural support measures. In case of conflict, these special rules prevail over the rules of SCM Agreement (Article 21.1 of the Agreement on Agriculture). In contrast to export subsidies on other products, export subsidies on agricultural products are not prohibited provided that they are specified in Section II of Part IV of a Member's Goods Schedule. These export subsidies are subject to reduction commitments. Members may not provide listed export subsidies in excess of the annual budgetary outlay and quantitative commitment levels specified in their Goods Schedules (Article 8 of the Agreement on Agriculture).

Also with respect to domestic agricultural support measures, Members have agreed to reduce their level of support, expressed as their 'aggregate measurement of support' (AMS). Under Article 6.3 of the Agreement on Agriculture, Members may not provide domestic support in excess of their AMS reduction commitments, as set out in Part IV of their Goods Schedules. The Agreement on Agriculture exempts from the AMS reduction commitments certain categories of domestic agricultural support measures that do not provide price support to agricultural producers. These support measures are known as 'green box' subsidies and 'blue box' subsidies. Green box subsidies are those that have no, or at most minimal, trade-distorting effect and that meet the policy-specific criteria set out in Annex 2 of the Agreement on Agriculture. Green box subsidies include *inter alia* payments for general services, public stockholding for food security purposes, domestic food aid, payments for relief from natural disasters, structural adjustment programmes, payments under environmental programmes and payments under regional assistance programmes. 'Blue box' subsidies are certain developing-country subsidies that are designed to encourage agricultural and rural development, subsidies below certain *de minimis* levels and certain payments aimed at limiting agricultural production. The conditions that these 'blue box' subsidies have to meet are set out in Articles 6.2, 6.4 and 6.5 of the Agreement on Agriculture.

Further reading

Dumping

Bown, P. C., and Mavroidis, C. P. (2013) 'One (firm) is not enough: a legal–economic analysis of EC–Fasteners', *World Trade Review* 12 243–271.

Dunoff L. J., and Moore, O. M. (2014) 'Footloose and duty-free? Reflections on European Union – Anti-Dumping Measures on Certain Footwear from China', *World Trade Review* 13 149–178.

Durling, J. P. (2003) 'Deference, but only when due: WTO review of anti-dumping measures', *Journal of International Economic Law* 6 (1) 125–153.

Subsidization

Charnowitz, S., and Fischer, C. (2015) 'Canada–Renewable Energy: implications for WTO law on green and not-so-green subsidies', *World Trade Review* 14 177–210.

Cosbey, A., and Mavroidis, C. P. (2014) 'A turquoise mess: green subsidies, blue industrial policy and renewable energy: the case for redrafting the Subsidies Agreement of the WTO', *Journal of International Economic Law*, 17 11–47.

Hahn, M., and Mehta, K. (2013) 'It's a bird, it's a plane: some remarks on the Airbus Appellate Body report (EC and certain member States – Large Civil Aircraft, WT/DS316/AB/R)', *World Trade Review* 12 139–161.

Pauwelyn, J. (2013) 'Treaty interpretation or activism? Comment on the AB report on United States – ADs and CVDs on Certain Products from China', *World Trade Review* 12 235–241.

Prusa, J. T., and Vermulst, E. (2013) 'United States – Definitive Anti-Dumping and Countervailing Duties on Certain Products from China: passing the buck on pass-through', *World Trade Review* 12 197–234.

Rubini, L. (2012) '"wastin' time no more". Subsidies for renewable energy, the SCM Agreement, policy space and law reform', *Journal of International Economic Law* 15(2) 525–579.

Chapter 6

Rules regarding harmonization of national regulation

6.1 Introduction

As customs duties and quotas decrease in importance as barriers to trade in goods, regulatory barriers to trade gain steadily in significance. Technical regulations and standards, as well as sanitary and phytosanitary measures, can pose significant obstacles to trade and may be misused to protect domestic products against competition from imported products. The TBT Agreement and the SPS Agreement aim to prevent such misuse and to minimize the trade-restrictive impact of legitimate regulation. Also, the lack of protection of intellectual property (IP) rights negatively affects trade in goods and services. Therefore, the TRIPS Agreement aims to ensure that the relevant regulations of WTO Members provide a minimum level of effective protection of IP rights.

The three WTO agreements mentioned here, the TBT Agreement, the SPS Agreement and the TRIPS Agreement, have an important aspect in common. Their obligations regarding national regulation go *beyond* the general rules of the GATT 1994 applicable to non-tariff barriers to trade, which address such measures primarily by prohibiting them (as is the case for quantitative restrictions; see Section 3.4) or by requiring their non-discriminatory application (as is the case for internal taxes and regulations; see Sections 2.2

and 2.4). The TBT Agreement, the SPS Agreement, and the TRIPS Agreement go further than this and promote the harmonization of national regulation on the basis of international standards or rules.

6.2 The TBT Agreement

WTO Members have many regulatory requirements in place regarding products that are traded in their territories; for instance, on the composition, quality, safety, production process, packaging and labelling of these products. Such requirements are commonly aimed at achieving legitimate public policy objectives, such as the protection of public health, the environment, consumers or public morals. However, because these regulatory requirements often differ from country to country, and products not meeting the specific requirements of the domestic market are banned, they may constitute formidable barriers to trade. They are also vulnerable to misuse for protectionist purposes. The TBT Agreement imposes disciplines on these technical requirements.

6.2.1 *Scope of application*

The TBT Agreement applies to:

- technical regulations;
- standards; and
- conformity assessment procedures.

According to Annex 1.1 of the TBT Agreement and the relevant case law, a measure is a *technical regulation* if:

- the measure applies to an identifiable product or group of products;
- the measure lays down product characteristics or their related processes and production methods; and
- compliance with the measure is mandatory.

The obligations applicable to technical regulations are set out in Articles 2 and 3 of the TBT Agreement.

A *standard* differs from a technical regulation within the meaning of the TBT Agreement on one important point; in contrast to a technical regulation, compliance with a standard is not mandatory (see Annex 1.2 of the TBT Agreement). Nevertheless, standards can have a significant impact on trade because there may be very strong incentives for compliance. The rules specifically applicable to standards are set out in Article 4 of and Annex 3 to the TBT Agreement. Annex 3 contains the Code of Good Practice for the Preparation, Adoption and Application of Standards (Code of Good Practice).

A *conformity assessment procedure*, according to Annex 1.3 of the TBT Agreement, is a procedure, such as inspection, sampling or testing, used to verify compliance with the requirements set out in technical regulations or standards. The rules applicable to conformity assessment procedures can be found in Articles 5, 6, 7, 8 and 9 of the TBT Agreement.

Industria has a number of technical rules in place with regard to smartphones. In particular (1) Industria's Electromagnetic Compatibility Act requires that smartphones be designed and manufactured according to certain technical specifications that ensure that the electromagnetic disturbance generated by the use of these phones does not exceed the level above which radio and telecommunications equipment or other equipment cannot operate as intended; (2) smartphone manufacturers are required to perform an electromagnetic compatibility assessment of the phones they produce in all normal intended operating conditions, on the basis of conformity with the relevant specifications of the Electromagnetic Compatibility Act (such conformity is certified by the manufacturer by affixing the 'IE' mark on the relevant smart phones); and (3) Industria's Committee for Electrotechnical Standardization has developed a voluntary mobile wireless standard for the incorporation of fifth-generation (5G) cellular technologies in smartphones. All three of these measures fall within the scope of application of the TBT Agreement because they fall within the definitions of a technical regulation, a conformity assessment procedure and a standard, respectively.

There is some debate whether requirements regarding the process and production method (PPM) whereby a product is made are covered by the TBT Agreement when such PPM does not affect the characteristics of the final product. Examples of such non–product-related PPM requirements are rules prescribing that the production process of a product comply with minimum labour conditions, maximum carbon emission levels or animal welfare requirements.

According to the Appellate Body in *EC – Seal Products (2014)*, the term 'their related processes and production methods' requires that the PPMs prescribed by the measure at issue have 'a sufficient nexus to the characteristics of a product in order to be considered *related* to those characteristics'. Note, however, that the Appellate Body stated that drawing the line between PPMs that fall, and those that do not fall, within the scope of the TBT Agreement raises 'important systemic issues' and did not further address the issue in *EC – Seal Products (2014)*.

Note that with regard to measures dealing with 'terminology, symbols, packaging, marking or labelling requirements', the adjective 'related' is absent in the definitions of a technical regulation and a standard (see second sentence of Annex 1.1 [concerning technical regulations] and second sentence of Annex 1.2 [concerning standards]). Therefore marking or labelling requirements relating to non–product-related PPMs are covered by the definitions in Annex 1 to the TBT Agreement and thus fall within the scope of application of the TBT Agreement.

The labelling requirements at issue in *US – COOL (2012)* and *US – Tuna II (Mexico) (2012)* both related to non–product-related PPMs (a requirement that beef and pork be labelled by retailers to indicate the country of birth, raising and slaughter of the animals from which the meat was derived and a measure setting out the requirements for the use of a 'dolphin-safe' label on tuna products, respectively). In both cases, the respondent, the United States, accepted that the labelling requirements at issue fell within the scope of application of the TBT Agreement.

Not only central government bodies but also local government bodies and, increasingly, non-governmental bodies are active in setting technical requirements for products and assessing conformity with such requirements. For this reason, although the TBT Agreement is mainly addressed to central government bodies, it extends its application also to local government and non-governmental bodies (Articles 3.1, 3.4, 4.1 and 8 of the TBT Agreement). WTO Members must (1) take 'such reasonable measures as may be available to them' in order to ensure compliance with the TBT Agreement by local government and non-governmental bodies, and (2) refrain from taking measures that could encourage actions by these bodies that are inconsistent with the provisions of the TBT Agreement.

With regard to the relationship between the TBT Agreement and other WTO agreements, note that, generally speaking, the applicability of the Agreement on Government Procurement or the SPS Agreement to a specific measure excludes the applicability of the TBT Agreement to that measure (Articles 1.4 and 1.5 of the TBT Agreement). By contrast, the TBT Agreement and the GATT 1994 can both be applicable to a specific measure. In case of conflict, the TBT Agreement prevails (General Interpretative Note to Annex 1A of the WTO Agreement).

6.2.2 Substantive obligations

The TBT Agreement requires that Members accord national treatment and most favoured-nation (MFN) treatment to imported products in respect of their technical regulations (Article 2.1 of the TBT Agreement), standards (Annex 3.D to the TBT Agreement) and conformity assessment procedures (Article 5.1.1 of the TBT Agreement).

With regard to technical regulations, Article 2.1 of the TBT Agreement has been interpreted as setting out a three-tier test of consistency with the national treatment obligation and the MFN treatment obligation. This test of consistency requires the examination of whether:

- the measure at issue is a 'technical regulation' within the meaning of Annex 1.1;
- the imported and domestic products (for the national treatment obligation) or the imported products originating in different countries (for the MFN treatment obligation) are 'like products'; and
- the imported products at issue are accorded 'treatment no less favourable' than like domestic products or than like imported products originating in other countries.

With regard to the first element of this test, please refer to the discussion of the definition of a 'technical regulation' in Section 6.2.1. The second element, that of 'like products', is in essence a determination about the nature and extent of the competitive relationship between and among the products at issue, as is the case for the national treatment and MFN treatment obligations in the GATT 1994 (see Section 2.2.3).

In *US – Clove Cigarettes (2012)* the panel held that the concept of 'likeness' in Article 2.1 of the TBT Agreement should be interpreted as focusing on the objectives and purposes of the technical regulation (*in casu* the regulation of flavoured cigarettes for public health reasons), rather than on the competitive relationship between the products. The Appellate Body rejected the panel's purpose-based approach to the determination of 'likeness' under Article 2.1 and chose to follow the competition-based approach to 'likeness' applicable under the GATT 1994. However, the Appellate Body did recognize that the regulatory concerns underlying a measure, such as the health risks associated with the product, may be relevant to the determination of 'likeness' (under both Article III:4 of the GATT 1994 and Article 2.1 of the TBT Agreement), to the extent that they have an impact on the competitive relationship between and among the products concerned.

The third element of the test, that of 'less favourable treatment', is, in the first place, a determination of the existence of a detrimental impact on the competitive conditions in the relevant market between the like products compared, as is the case for the 'less favourable treatment' test of Article III:4 of the GATT 1994 (see Section 2.4.3.3). However, whereas a detrimental impact on the competitive conditions is suffi-cient to establish 'less favourable treatment' under Article III:4 of the GATT 1994, it is *not sufficient* to establish a violation of Article 2.1 of the TBT Agreement in cases of de facto discriminatory treatment. In such cases, it is necessary to further determine whether the detrimental impact on compe-titive conditions 'stems exclusively from a legitimate regula-tory distinction' rather than reflecting discrimination against a group of imported products.

The Appellate Body in *US – Clove Cigarettes (2012)* interpreted the term 'treatment no less favourable' in Article 2.1 of the TBT Agreement in this way on the basis of its context and the object and purpose of the TBT Agreement. In particular, although the TBT Agreement does not contain a general exceptions clause similar to Article XX of the GATT 1994, the sixth recital of the Preamble to the TBT Agreement recognizes that 'no country should be prevented from taking mea-sures necessary' to pursue policy objectives such as the protection of public health, the protection of the environment and the protection of the consumer. The Appellate Body noted that the object and purpose of the TBT Agreement is to strike a balance between the objective of trade liberalization and a WTO Member's right to regulate. Thus, the 'treatment no less

> favourable' requirement of Article 2.1 was interpreted as 'prohibiting both *de jure* and *de facto* discrimination against imported products, while at the same time permitting detrimental impact on competitive opportunities for imports that stems exclusively from legitimate regulatory distinctions'.

To establish whether detrimental impact on competitive opportunities stems exclusively from a legitimate regulatory distinction, it is necessary to carefully examine the 'design, architecture, revealing structure, operation, and application of the technical regulation at issue, and, in particular, whether that technical regulation is even-handed'. If a regulatory distinction is designed or applied in a way that is not even-handed (e.g. where it is designed or applied in a manner that constitutes arbitrary or unjustifiable discrimination), it will not be considered 'legitimate', and the detrimental impact will thus amount to discrimination, contrary to Article 2.1 of the TBT Agreement.

> In *US – Clove Cigarettes (2012)*, the measure at issue was a US ban on clove cigarettes and other flavoured cigarettes, with the exception of menthol cigarettes. Because the vast majority of clove cigarettes consumed in the United States came from Indonesia, whereas almost all menthol cigarettes consumed in the United States were domestically produced, the Appellate Body held that the design, architecture, revealing structure, operation and application of the measure at issue strongly

suggested that the detrimental impact on competitive opportunities for clove cigarettes reflected discrimination against the group of like products imported from Indonesia. Moreover, the Appellate Body was not convinced that the detrimental impact on competitive opportunities for imported clove cigarettes stemmed from a legitimate regulatory distinction.

Although there is no relevant case law yet, it is likely that similar tests of consistency will be found to apply, *mutatis mutandis*, with regard to the national treatment and MFN treatment obligation applicable to standards and to conformity assessment procedures.

The TBT Agreement further requires that technical regulations, standards and conformity assessment procedures do not create unnecessary obstacles to international trade. To this end, Article 2.2 of the TBT Agreement requires that technical regulations not be more trade-restrictive than necessary to fulfil a legitimate objective, taking account of the risks non-fulfilment would create. It provides a non-exhaustive list of such legitimate objectives, namely the prevention of deceptive practices, national security requirements, and the protection of human health or safety, animal or plant life or health, or the environment. Article 2.2 contains a four-tier test of consistency, namely:

- whether the measure at issue is a 'technical regulation' within the meaning of Annex 1.1;
- whether the measure at issue is 'trade-restrictive';

- whether the measure at issue fulfils a legitimate objective; and
- whether the measure at issue is 'not more trade-restrictive than necessary' to fulfil the legitimate objective, taking account of the risks non-fulfilment would create.

The fourth element of this test requires an assessment resembling the 'necessity' test of Article XX(a), (b) or (d) of the GATT 1994 (Section 4.2.1).

The Appellate Body in *US – Tuna II (Mexico) (2012)* clarified the determination of whether a technical regulation is 'not more trade-restrictive than necessary' as required by Article 2.2. It held that a panel should start by conducting a 'relational analysis' of factors including (1) the degree of contribution made by the measure to the legitimate objective at issue, (2) the trade-restrictiveness of the measure and (3) the nature of the risks at issue and the gravity of consequences that would arise from non-fulfilment of the objective(s) pursued by the Member through the measure. In most cases, this analysis should be followed by a comparison of the challenged measure and possible alternative measures that are reasonably available (the 'comparative analysis').

Standards and conformity assessment procedures are subject to similar obligations (Annex 3.E and Article 5.1.2 of the TBT Agreement).

The most innovative aspect of the TBT Agreement is its promotion of harmonization of technical regulations, standards and conformity assessment procedures on the basis of international standards. For purposes of the TBT Agreement, international standards are those adopted by international standardizing bodies (i.e. bodies with recognized activities in standardization that are open on a non-discriminatory basis to relevant bodies of at least all WTO Members). International standards need not be adopted by consensus. With regard to technical regulations, Article 2.4 of the TBT Agreement sets out a three-tier test of consistency, namely:

- whether a relevant international standard exists or is imminent;
- whether the international standard is 'used as a basis' (i.e. used as the principal constituent or fundamental principle) for the technical regulation; and
- whether the international standard would be an effective and appropriate means for the fulfilment of the legitimate objectives pursued by the Member.

If, for example, due to specific climatic or geographic conditions, the international standard is ineffective or inappropriate to fulfil the Member's legitimate objective, the technical regulation need not be based on the international standard. Note that if a technical regulation is in accordance with the relevant international standards and pursues one of the legitimate objectives expressly listed in Article 2.2, then it is rebuttably presumed not to create an unnecessary obstacle to international trade (Article 2.5 of the TBT Agreement). Similar harmonization obligations apply to standards and conformity assessment procedures (Annex 3.F and Article 5.4 of the TBT Agreement).

In *EC – Sardines (2002)*, an EC Regulation prohibiting the identification or marketing of preserved fish products other than *Sardina pilchardus* as 'sardines' was challenged in terms of Article 2.4 of the TBT Agreement. The Appellate Body held that Codex Stan-94 did not have to be adopted by consensus for it to be the relevant 'international standard' on which the EC Regulation should have been based. Furthermore, the Appellate Body regarded Codex Stan-94 as the 'relevant' international standard as it 'related to' or was 'pertinent to' the EC Regulation because both related to the species *Sardina pilchardus* and had implications for which preserved fish species could be marketed as 'sardines'. The Appellate Body found that the EC Regulation did not use Codex Stan-94 'as a basis' because it contradicted this international standard by prohibiting the use of the name 'sardines' for several species of preserved fish that Codex Stan-94 allowed to be marketed under this name. Finally, noting the three objectives of the EC Regulation at issue (market transparency, consumer protection and fair competition), the Appellate Body held that Codex Stan 94 was 'effective' (had the capacity to accomplish the objectives) and 'appropriate' (was suitable for the fulfillment of the objectives). The EC Regulation was therefore found to violate Article 2.4 of the TBT Agreement.

The TBT Agreement also requires WTO Members to give *positive consideration* to accepting as equivalent the different technical regulations and conformity assessment procedures of other WTO Members if these measures adequately fulfil the objectives of their own measures (Articles 2.7 and 6.1 of the TBT Agreement).

Furthermore, the TBT Agreement imposes far-reaching transparency obligations. These obligations include provisions on advance notification of draft technical regulations, with the provision of a comment period, except in cases of urgent safety, health, environmental protection or national security problems (Articles 2.9, 2.10 of the TBT Agreement). In addition, Article 2.11 of the TBT Agreement requires that Members promptly publish all adopted technical regulations. Except when a technical regulation addresses an *urgent* problem, Members must allow a reasonable interval between the publication of a technical regulation and its entry into force in order to allow foreign producers to adapt to the new requirements (Article 2.12 of the TBT Agreement). This 'reasonable interval' was clarified in the Doha Ministerial Decision on Implementation-Related Issues and Concerns as normally not less than six months, except when this would be ineffective in fulfilling the legitimate objectives pursued. Similar transparency obligations apply to standards (Annex 3.L, M, N and O to the TBT Agreement) and conformity assessment procedures (Articles 5.6, 5.7, 5.8 and 5.9 of the TBT Agreement).

Finally, the TBT Agreement provides for technical assistance and special and differential (S&D) treatment for developing-country Members (Articles 11 and 12 of the TBT Agreement). *Inter alia*, Members must 'take into account' the 'special development, financial and trade needs' of developing-country Members in the implementation of the TBT Agreement and in the preparation and application of technical regulations, standards and conformity assessment procedures (Articles 12.2 and 12.3 of the TBT Agreement). However, as with most other S&D treatment provisions, these are worded in a manner that is difficult to enforce.

In *US – COOL (2012)*, Mexico claimed that the United States had violated its obligation under Article 12.3 to 'take account of [Mexico's] special development, financial and trade needs' in the preparation and application of the country of origin (COOL) measure. The panel, however, did not consider that the United States 'had an explicit obligation, enforceable in WTO dispute settlement, to reach out and collect Mexico's views during the preparation and application of the COOL measure'. According to the panel, the obligation to 'take account of' Mexico's needs means 'giving active and meaningful consideration to such needs'.

6.2.3 *Institutional and procedural provisions*

Article 13.1 of the TBT Agreement establishes the TBT Committee, composed of representatives of all WTO Members. Its function is to provide Members with a forum for consultations regarding any matters pertaining to the operation or objectives of the TBT Agreement. Members regularly discuss their 'specific trade concerns' with regard to the measures of other Members at meetings of the TBT

Committee. The TBT Committee also carries out annual and triennial reviews of the operation of the TBT Agreement (Articles 15.3 and 15.4 of the TBT Agreement). It has further adopted certain decisions and recommendations to further the implementation of the TBT Agreement.

Disputes arising under the TBT Agreement are in general subject to the normal dispute settlement procedures set out in the Dispute Settlement Understanding (DSU) (see Chapter 8).

6.3 The SPS Agreement

In WTO law, a specific category of measures can be identified within the general category of technical barriers to trade, namely sanitary and phytosanitary measures (SPS measures). SPS measures are, *broadly speaking*, measures that aim to protect human, animal or plant life or health from risks arising from pests or diseases of plants or animals or from food safety risks. Fumigation requirements to eliminate fruit flies on imported apples, maximum residue levels for pesticides on vegetables and restrictions on poultry imports from countries where avian flu is prevalent are examples of SPS measures. These measures were considered to merit special treatment in a separate agreement due to the very sensitive nature of the conflicting interests at stake; namely, the protection of health, on the one hand, and the liberalization of trade in primary and processed agricultural products, on the other. The Agreement on the Application of Sanitary and Phytosanitary Measures (SPS Agreement) imposes disciplines on this category of measures that aim to balance these completing interests.

6.3.1 Scope of application

The SPS Agreement applies to 'SPS measures' that directly or indirectly affect international trade. The definition of an 'SPS measure' in Annex A.1 of the SPS Agreement focuses on the *purpose* of the measure. An 'SPS measure' is a measure that aims at:

- the protection of human or animal life or health from risks in food or feed;
- the protection of human, animal or plant life or health from risks from pests or diseases carried by plants or animals; or
- the prevention or limitation of 'other damage' from pests.

Note that the definition in Annex A(1) refers explicitly to the protection of human, animal or plant life or health or the prevention of other damage 'within the territory of the Member'. Therefore, measures aiming at extraterritorial health protection are expressly excluded from the scope of application of the SPS Agreement.

> The Appellate Body in *Australia – Apples (2010)*, emphasized that the fundamental element of the definition of an 'SPS measure' relates to the *purpose* or *intention* of the measure and that this 'is to be ascertained on the basis of objective considerations'. Thus, the purpose of the measure is determined 'not only from the objectives of the measure as expressed by the responding party, but also from the text and structure of the relevant measure, its surrounding regulatory context, and the way in which it is designed and applied'.

The definition of an 'SPS measure' includes an open, illustrative list of the types of instruments (such as laws, regulations and requirements) that may be SPS measures if they meet the purpose criterion of that definition.

Although primarily central government bodies adopt and apply SPS measures, and Members are fully responsible for compliance of these bodies with the SPS Agreement, in some cases local government bodies, regional bodies and non-governmental bodies (such as regulatory agencies or national bureaus of standards) may also adopt or apply SPS measures. In respect of such bodies, Article 13 of the SPS Agreement requires Members to take 'such reasonable measures as may be available to them' to ensure compliance with the SPS Agreement, and it prohibits them from directly or indirectly encouraging non-compliance. It is much debated whether these obligations on Members extend to the actions of private-sector entities imposing SPS-related standards, such as retailers (e.g. Tesco's Nature's Choice) or non-governmental organizations (e.g. GlobalGAP). There are ongoing discussions on this issue in the SPS Committee.

Clearly, not only the SPS Agreement is of relevance for trade-restrictive measures that aim to protect health. The GATT 1994 and the TBT Agreement also may apply to such measures. However, as noted in Section 6.2.1, the TBT Agreement does not apply to measures falling within the definition of an 'SPS measure' in Annex A.1 of the SPS Agreement, even if the SPS measure at issue takes the form of technical regulation, standard or conformity assessment procedure. Note, however, that a measure may pursue multiple objectives, some falling within the definition of an 'SPS measure' and others not. In such cases, to the extent that the measure pursues a non-SPS objective, it may be covered by the TBT Agreement.

In *EC – Approval and Marketing of Biotech Products (2006)*, one of the measures at issue, the EC regulation on novel foods, aimed at protecting human health against food-safety risks as well as ensuring consumer information. The panel recognized that a single measure may have both an SPS objective and a non-SPS objective, in which case it would need to be assessed under both the SPS Agreement and, if it complies with the definition of a 'technical regulation', the TBT Agreement.

There is no relationship of mutual exclusivity between the SPS Agreement and the GATT 1994. However, Article 2.4 of the SPS Agreement provides that a measure complying with the SPS Agreement is presumed to comply with the relevant provisions of the GATT 1994. This presumption is rebuttable.

6.3.2 *Obligations and requirements*

The SPS Agreement, in Article 2.1, explicitly acknowledges the sovereign right of WTO Members to take SPS measures to protect human, animal or plant life or health in their territories. At the same time, however, the SPS Agreement subjects Members who make use of this right to certain obligations, incorporating existing GATT rules applicable to health measures and introducing new requirements for the use of SPS measures.

According to Article 2.2, WTO Members may only apply SPS measures to the extent necessary for the protection of human, animal or plant life or health. This basic requirement is elaborated on in Article 5.6 of the SPS Agreement (discussed later).

Furthermore, Article 2.2 requires that SPS measures be based on scientific principles and not be maintained without sufficient scientific evidence, except as provided for in Article 5.7 (discussed later). This provision introduces science as the benchmark against which SPS measures are judged and is further elaborated on in Article 5.1, which requires that SPS measures be based on a 'risk assessment', as discussed later.

> The key role of the scientific requirements of the SPS Agreement was stressed by the Appellate Body in *EC – Hormones (1998)*, which stated that '[t]he requirements of a risk assessment under Article 5.1, as well as of "sufficient scientific evidence" under Article 2.2, are essential for the maintenance of the delicate and carefully negotiated balance in the SPS Agreement between the shared, but sometimes competing, interests of promoting international trade and of protecting the life and health of human beings'.

Article 2.3 contains the obligations of national treatment and MFN treatment. It prohibits WTO Members from imposing SPS measures that arbitrarily or unjustifiably discriminate between Members where identical or similar conditions prevail or that constitute a disguised restriction on trade.

For a violation of Article 2.3, a three-tier test applies, namely:

- the measure discriminates between the territories of Members other than the Member imposing the measure, or between the territory of the Member imposing the measure and another Member;
- the discrimination is arbitrary or unjustifiable; and
- identical or similar conditions prevail in the territory of the Members compared.

Note with regard to the first element of this test that, by contrast with the non-discrimination obligations of the GATT (Sections 2.2 and 2.4), the discrimination prohibited by Article 2.3 of the SPS Agreement includes discrimination between products that are not 'like' or 'directly competitive or substitutable'. What is of relevance under Article 2.3 is the similarity of the relevant *health risks*. One could think here of the possibility that different chemicals may be equally carcinogenic, diverse fruits may be vectors for fruit flies or various bird species can be carriers of avian flu. Although potentially very broad, the scope of this non-discrimination obligation is limited by the second and third elements of the three-tier test. If the discrimination is not arbitrary or unjustifiable, or if the conditions prevailing in the Members at issue are dissimilar, Article 2.3 is not violated.

In *Australia – Salmon (Article 21.5 – Canada) (2000)* the issue arose whether the fact that Australia imposed import requirements on salmonids from Canada but provided no internal control measures on the movement of dead domestic fish constituted a violation of Article 2.3 of the SPS Agreement. The panel recognized that the prohibition in Article 2.3 includes discrimination between different products, in this case salmonids from Canada and dead domestic fish products. The panel also found that both categories of products at issue entailed the risk of entry, establishment or spread of the same or similar fish diseases. However, the panel was not convinced that 'identical or similar' conditions prevailed in Australia and Canada due to the 'substantial difference' in the disease status of these two Members.

The basic non-discrimination obligation of Article 2.3 is elaborated on in Article 5.5 of the SPS Agreement (discussed later).

Like the TBT Agreement, the SPS Agreement promotes harmonization on the basis of international standards. 'International standards' for purposes of the SPS Agreement are standards set by international organizations such as the Codex Alimentarius Commission with respect to food safety, the World Organisation for Animal Health with respect to animal health, and the Secretariat of the International Plant Protection Convention with respect to plant health. Unlike the TBT Agreement, Article 3 of the SPS

Agreement provides Members with three *autonomous* (i.e. equally available) options with regard to international standards, each with its own consequences. Members may choose to:

- impose SPS measures that are '*based* on' (i.e. built upon/ supported by) international standards (Article 3.1);
- impose SPS measures that '*conform* to' (i.e. completely embody) international standards (Article 3.2); or
- impose SPS measures that result in a *higher level* of protection than would be achieved by the relevant international standard (Article 3.3).

A Member that chooses the second option benefits from a rebuttable presumption of consistency of its SPS measure with the SPS Agreement and the GATT 1994. This gives Members an incentive to adopt harmonized SPS measures. A Member that chooses the third option, and thus deviates from the relevant international standard, must have a scientific justification for its measure in the form of a risk assessment as required by Article 5.1.

Cadmium, a heavy metal that is taken up naturally from the soil by cocoa plants, is known to cause kidney damage and increase the risk of cancer. The Codex Alimentarius Commission, in Codex Stan-87, has set a maximum residue level of 2.5 μg/kg for cadmium in chocolate to address this risk. Consumers in Industria are very risk-averse when it comes to children's health. Industria has decided to deviate from Codex Stan-87

---

and ban chocolate containing any cadmium residues. This is due to its concerns for the safety of Industria's children, who eat large quantities of chocolate. Industria is free to do so, if it can demonstrate that its ban is based on a risk assessment, as required by Article 5.1 of the SPS Agreement.

As already mentioned, the obligations set out in Articles 2.2 and 2.3 of the SPS Agreement are further specified and elaborated on in a number of other provisions containing substantive obligations relating to the risk analysis process that underlies national SPS regulation. Risk analysis encompasses risk assessment (i.e. the process of identifying a risk and establishing the chance that it will materialize) and risk management (i.e. the choice of an appropriate level of protection against the identified risk *and* of an SPS measure to achieve this level of protection).

With regard to risk assessment, Article 5.1 of the SPS Agreement requires that SPS measures be 'based on' (i.e. have a rational relationship with) a risk assessment, as appropriate to the circumstances. Annex A(4) provides definitions for two types of risk assessment: one for risks from pests and diseases and one for risks from food and feed. The requirements of the former are less strict than of the latter, but neither requires a quantification of risk. Instead, risk may be established quantitatively or qualitatively, and no minimum threshold of risk is required. A non-exhaustive list of factors that Members must take into account in conducting a risk assessment is provided in Article 5.2.

> In *EC – Hormones (1998)*, the Appellate Body overturned the panel's finding that risks relating to problems of control in ensuring good veterinary practices in the administration of veterinary drugs must be excluded from the factors to be considered in undertaking a risk assessment according to Article 5.2 because they are non-scientific. According to the Appellate Body, a risk assessment is not limited to laboratory science but must take into account risks in the 'real world where people live and work and die'.

Note that a risk assessment may reflect not only mainstream scientific opinion, but also a divergent minority scientific opinion provided it comes from a qualified and respected source (i.e. the views must be regarded as legitimate science according to the standards of the relevant scientific community). Also, Members need not conduct their own risk assessments but are free to base their SPS measures on risk assessments carried out in other Members or by international organizations.

> Although mainstream scientific opinion regards 2.5 µg/kg of cadmium in chocolate as a safe level, a small group of eminent Alpinian scientists have recently conducted a study, published in a peer-reviewed scientific journal, concluding that children's kidneys are particularly susceptible to damage from cadmium, even at very low levels, if regularly consumed. Industria may rely on this 'borrowed' minority risk assessment as a basis for its ban on chocolate containing any residues of cadmium.

Despite its focus on science as the benchmark against which Member's SPS measures are judged, the SPS Agreement takes into account the fact that situations may arise in which there is some indication that a risk exists, but a risk assessment is impossible due to the lack of sufficient scientific evidence. In such situations, Members may consider that they need to act promptly and thus take measures to avoid possible harm without waiting for the collection of sufficient scientific information to assess the risks conclusively (known as 'acting in accordance with the precautionary principle'). The SPS Agreement allows such precautionary action by providing, in Article 5.7, a qualified exemption from its science-based obligations.

In *US/Canada – Continued Suspension (2008)*, the Appellate Body noted that Article 5.7 provides '[a] temporary "safety valve" in situations where some evidence of risk exists but not enough to complete a full risk assessment, thus making it impossible to meet the rigorous standards set by Articles 2.2 and 5.1'.

Article 5.7 of the SPS Agreement allows Members to take provisional SPS measures where such measures are:

- imposed in respect of a situation where relevant scientific evidence is insufficient to allow a risk assessment to be conducted;
- adopted on the basis of available pertinent information, indicating the possible existence of a risk;

- not maintained unless the Member seeks to obtain the additional information necessary for a more objective assessment of risk; and
- reviewed within a reasonable period of time.

In *Japan – Apples (2003)*, the United States challenged a range of requirements imposed by Japan to prevent the introduction into its territory of fire-blight, a bacterium that infects apple trees and causes them to wither and die. Japan argued that the existence of 'scientific uncertainty' regarding the transmission of fire-blight triggered the applicability of Article 5.7 of the SPS Agreement. The panel disagreed, holding that '[t]he current "situation", where scientific studies as well as practical experience have accumulated for the past 200 years, is clearly not the type of situation Article 5.7 was intended to address. Article 5.7 was obviously designed to be invoked in situations where little, or no, reliable evidence was available on the subject-matter at issue'. The Appellate Body agreed with the panel, clarifying that Article 5.7 'is triggered not by the existence of scientific uncertainty, but rather by the insufficiency of scientific evidence'. It held that relevant scientific evidence will be 'insufficient' within the meaning of Article 5.7 if it 'does not allow, in qualitative or quantitative terms, the performance of an adequate assessment of risks as required under Article 5.1'.

With regard to risk management (i.e. the policy-based process of choosing a level of protection against an SPS risk *and* a measure to achieve this level of protection), the SPS Agreement gives Members substantial latitude. It recognizes the prerogative of each Member to set its own 'appropriate level of protection' against SPS risks. However, Members must:

- 'take into account' the *objective* of minimizing negative trade effects (Article 5.4); and
- avoid arbitrary or unjustifiable distinctions in the levels of protection deemed appropriate in different situations, if these distinctions lead to discrimination or disguised restrictions on trade (Article 5.5).

Although the first of these obligations is rather weak, the second sets out an enforceable obligation. The Appellate Body has clarified that the obligation of Article 5.5 does not require 'absolute consistency' in levels of protection, recognizing that countries establish their levels of protection ad hoc as risks arise. Only *arbitrary* or *unjustifiable* distinctions in levels of protection which result in *discrimination* or *disguised restrictions* on trade are prohibited.

An SPS measure is inconsistent with Article 5.5 if:

- the Member concerned has set *different levels of protection* in different, but comparable, situations (i.e. situations with common elements such as those involving the same disease);
- these different levels of protection show *arbitrary or unjustifiable differences* in their treatment of different, but comparable, situations; and

- these arbitrary or unjustifiable differences lead to *discrimination* or *disguised restrictions* on trade.

As is the case in Article 2.3 of the SPS Agreement discussed earlier, for the discrimination relevant for purposes of Article 5.5, it is the similarity of the risks, rather than the similarity of the products, that matters.

The disciplines applicable to risk management in the SPS Agreement further include two obligations relevant to the choice of an SPS measure. Members must:

- consider, in choosing an SPS measure to address risks to plant/animal health, certain economic factors such as damage in terms of loss of production or sales and costs of control or eradication (Article 5.3); and
- ensure that their SPS measures are not more trade-restrictive than required to achieve their appropriate level of protection (Article 5.6).

The latter obligation can be seen as a further elaboration of the 'necessity' requirement of Article 2.2 of the SPS Agreement. A footnote to Article 5.6 clarifies that a measure is more trade-restrictive than required if there is an alternative measure that:

- is reasonably available, taking into account technical and economic feasibility;
- achieves the regulating Member's appropriate level of sanitary or phytosanitary protection; and
- is significantly less restrictive to trade than the SPS measure being applied.

Note that, under this test, any alternative must not only be significantly less trade restrictive and technically and economically feasible for the importing Member, but must also achieve its chosen level of protection from SPS risks. Consequently, in respect of the second element of this test, the Appellate Body has clarified that it entails the identification of both the appropriate level of protection of the importing Member and the level of protection that would be achieved by the alternative measure proposed by the complainant in order to permit a comparison between the two. If the level of protection achieved by the alternative measure meets or exceeds the appropriate level of protection of the importing Member (and the other two conditions in Article 5.6 are met), then the importing Member's SPS measure is more trade-restrictive than necessary to achieve its desired level of protection and thus inconsistent with Article 5.6.

In *India – Agricultural Products (2015)*, in which India's ban on poultry products to prevent the entry and spread of avian influenza (AI) was challenged by the United States, the Appellate Body held: 'Each WTO Member enjoys the right to specify its own appropriate level of protection, but is also subject to an implicit obligation to do so with sufficient precision as to enable the application of the provisions of the SPS Agreement, including Article 5.6. A WTO Member cannot, by failing to specify its appropriate level of protection, or by doing so in an insufficiently precise way, escape its obligations under the SPS Agreement'. Although a panel must accord weight to a respondent's articulation of its appropriate level of protection, this does not mean that it should completely defer to a respondent's characterization of its appropriate level of protection. In this case, the Appellate Body stated that the panel had correctly identified India's appropriate level of protection 'on the basis of the totality of the arguments and evidence on the record' as being 'very high or very conservative'.

The SPS Agreement further imposes an obligation on Members to recognize the equivalence of different SPS measures of other Members if the latter demonstrably achieve the importing Member's level of protection (Article 4). To facilitate the implementation of this underused provision, the SPS Committee adopted, in 2001, the Decision on Equivalence.

Because sanitary and phytosanitary conditions, such as pest and disease prevalence, can vary greatly within a country, Article 6.1 of the SPS Agreement requires Members to adapt their SPS measures to the regional conditions prevailing in other Members. Articles 6.2 and 6.3 'elaborate the specific characteristics' of this obligation by requiring Members to recognize the concepts of pest- and disease-free regions and regions of low pest and disease prevalence and by setting out the obligations of the importing and exporting Members in this regard.

In *India – Agricultural Products (2015)*, the panel noted that Article 6.2 does not prescribe the manner in which Members must 'recognize' the concepts of disease-free areas and areas of low disease prevalence. However, it found that, by imposing a prohibition on a country-wide basis, the measure at issue contradicted the requirement to recognize these concepts. The Appellate Body agreed with this ruling.

Guidelines for the implementation of Article 6 have been developed in the 2008 Regionalization Decision of the SPS Committee.

Members usually have procedures in place to check compliance of products with their SPS requirements. These SPS-related control, inspection and approval procedures can be in themselves significant barriers to market access. Article 8, together with Annex C of the SPS Agreement, aim to ensure that these procedures are not more lengthy and burdensome than is reasonable and necessary and do not discriminate against imports.

The SPS Agreement contains far-reaching transparency obligations, including advance notification and publication requirements similar to those of the TBT Agreement (see Section 6.2.2). These are contained in Article 7 and Annex B of the SPS Agreement.

Acknowledging the difficulties developing-country Members may face in complying with the SPS requirements of importing Members and in implementing their obligations under the SPS Agreement, provision is made in Article 10 for special and differential treatment of developing-country Members. Furthermore, in Article 9, Members agree 'to facilitate' the provision of technical assistance and are obliged 'to consider providing' technical assistance where their SPS measures require substantial investments from developing-country exporting Members. Just as is the case under the TBT Agreement (discussed in Section 6.2.2), the provisions on special and differential treatment and on technical assistance in the SPS Agreement are formulated in a manner that makes them difficult to enforce.

6.3.3 Institutional and procedural provisions

Article 12 of the SPS Agreement establishes the SPS Committee, composed of representatives of all WTO Members, to further the implementation of this agreement. It provides a forum for Members to discuss matters pertaining to the operation or objectives of the SPS Agreement, including their 'specific trade concerns' regarding SPS measures of other Members. Many concerns are resolved in this way, without recourse to dispute settlement. In 2014, the SPS Committee has also adopted a 'mediation procedure' to facilitate the resolution of specific SPS issues between Members. In addition, discussions in the SPS Committee have led to the adoption of decisions to improve the implementation of certain obligations in the SPS Agreement, such as those on the recognition of equivalence, adaptation to regional conditions, and transparency.

The normal WTO dispute settlement procedures (discussed in Chapter 8) apply to disputes arising under the

SPS Agreement. However, in the context of SPS disputes, specific issues have arisen regarding:

- the appointment and use made of scientific experts by panels and
- the standard of review to be applied by panels.

Because highly complex issues of scientific evidence arise in SPS disputes, Article 11 of the SPS Agreement authorizes panels to consult experts. The selection and use of experts by panels has been rather controversial. The Appellate Body has clarified that, in the selection of panel experts, panels must ensure their independence and impartiality. The Appellate Body has also explained that the role of panel experts is to assist panels in understanding the factual evidence before them, not to help to make the case for one of the parties or to answer legal questions before the panel.

Similarly contentious has been the issue of the standard of review to be applied by panels when assessing compliance with the obligation to base SPS measures on a risk assessment, as required in Article 5.1 of the SPS Agreement (Section 6.3.2). The Appellate Body has distinguished two aspects of the review of a risk assessment:

- scrutiny of the underlying scientific basis and
- scrutiny of the reasoning of the risk assessor based on such underlying science.

In view of the fact that panels are not well-suited to conduct scientific assessments, the former should be limited to reviewing whether the scientific basis constitutes 'legitimate science according to the standards of the relevant scientific community'. However, the latter should be less deferential and involves an 'assessment of whether the reasoning of the risk assessor is objective and coherent, that is, whether the conclusions find sufficient support in the scientific evidence relied upon'.

Agricola has challenged Industria's low maximum residue levels for cadmium in chocolate on the basis of Article 5.1 of the SPS Agreement. Industria submits that its measure is based on a risk assessment conducted by a group of Alpinian scientists concluding that children's kidneys are particularly susceptible to damage from cadmium, even at very low levels, if regularly consumed. This conclusion was based on data gathered from scientific laboratory trials studying the effect of regular cadmium ingestion on the kidneys of young monkeys. The panel determining whether Industria has met its obligation under Article 5.1 of the SPS Agreement may only assess the data derived from the laboratory trials on monkeys to determine whether it constitutes 'legitimate science' by the standards of that scientific community. However, it may go further in its examination of the reasoning underlying the conclusions in the risk assessment regarding the risks of kidney damage to children and determine whether they are sufficiently supported by the scientific data generated by the laboratory trials and are thus objective and coherent.

6.4 The TRIPS Agreement

At first sight, the TRIPS Agreement seems to be a 'foreign element' in WTO law: whereas other WTO agreements address trade and trade regulation, the TRIPS Agreement focuses on the protection of IP rights. However, the lack of protection of IP rights can act as a barrier to trade because the economic value of many products (goods and services) is determined to a large extent by the idea and the knowledge reflected in the product and/or the reputation of the product or the producer. Without adequate protection of IP rights, such as copyright, patents and trademarks, the possibility that traded products will be copied or their brand names will be used by competitors may create a strong disincentive to trade. Also, disparities in national legislation for the protection of IP inhibit international trade. The TRIPS Agreement aims to address this problem by providing harmonized rules on minimum standards of IP protection.

A remarkable aspect of the TRIPS Agreement is the fact that it incorporates and builds upon provisions of existing conventions of the World Intellectual Property Organization (WIPO). Many provisions of the Paris Convention for the Protection of Industrial Property of 1967 (Paris Convention); the International Convention for the Protection of Performers, Producers of Phonograms and Broadcasting Organizations of 1961 (Rome Convention); the Treaty on Intellectual Property in respect of Integrated Circuits of 1989 (IPIC Treaty) and the Berne Convention for the Protection of Literary and Artistic Works of 1971

(Berne Convention) are an integral part of the TRIPS Agreement and must be respected by WTO Members. The obligations of the TRIPS Agreement must be read together with the incorporated WIPO conventions.

6.4.1 *Scope of application*

The protection of IP rights provided in the TRIPS Agreement must be granted by WTO Members to 'nationals' of other Members, which are understood to mean natural and legal persons who would meet the criteria for eligibility for protection set out in the incorporated WIPO conventions if all WTO Members were party to these conventions (Article 1.3 of the TRIPS Agreement).

The TRIPS Agreement does not define the concept of 'intellectual property' but instead specifies the categories of IP rights that are covered by its provisions. According to Article 1.2, these are those categories of IP rights that are the 'subject' of Sections 1 to 7 of Part II of the TRIPS Agreement. The Appellate Body has clarified that the coverage of the TRIPS Agreement is not limited to those IP rights *expressly* mentioned in these Sections of Part II, but includes also those in the incorporated WIPO conventions that are the 'subject' of these Sections. The most important categories of IP rights covered by the TRIPS Agreement are:

- copyright (such as the right of Dan Brown on *The Da Vinci Code*);
- trademarks (such as Nestle and iPhone);

- geographical indications (such as Prosciutto di Parma and Champagne); and
- patents (such as those on anti-retroviral medicines).

6.4.2 Basic principles and general provisions

The TRIPS Agreement not only provides for rules for the minimum protection of specific IP rights, but it also contains some generally applicable principles and obligations.

Article 7 of the TRIPS Agreement sets out the 'Objective' of the agreement, namely, the protection and enforcement of IP rights 'to contribute to the promotion of technological innovation and the transfer and dissemination of technology, to the mutual advantage of producers and users of technological knowledge and in a manner conducive to social and economic welfare, and to a balance of rights and obligations'. This balancing objective is further reflected in Article 8, entitled 'Principles', which recognizes that WTO Members may adopt measures 'necessary to protect public health and nutrition' and to 'promote the public interest in sectors of vital importance to their socio-economic and technological development' in a way *consistent* with the provisions of the TRIPS Agreement. This provision does not create an exception from the obligations of the TRIPS Agreement. Instead, as established in the Doha Declaration on the TRIPS Agreement and Public Health, the provisions of the TRIPS Agreement must be read in the light of the object and purpose of this Agreement as expressed in Articles 7 and 8.

Furthermore, Article 1.1 of the TRIPS Agreement establishes that although Members are obliged to give effect to the provisions of this Agreement, they are free to determine the appropriate method for implementing their obligations within their own legal systems. Members are also free to implement more extensive protection of IP rights than that required by the TRIPS Agreement.

In addition, the TRIPS Agreement contains a national treatment obligation and a MFN treatment obligation for the protection of IP rights. Whereas pre-existing WIPO conventions already incorporate a national treatment obligation, the TRIPS Agreement introduces for the first time an MFN treatment obligation in the area of IP protection.

As held by the Appellate Body in *US – Section 211 Appropriations Act (2002)*: 'As a cornerstone of the world trading system, the most-favoured-nation obligation must be accorded the same significance with respect to IP rights under the TRIPS Agreement that it has long been accorded with respect to trade in goods under the GATT. It is, in a word, fundamental'.

The obligations of national treatment and MFN treatment apply only to those categories of IP rights that are covered by the TRIPS Agreement. 'Protection' of IP rights is defined in footnote 3 to include 'matters affecting the availability, acquisition, scope, maintenance and enforcement' of those rights as well as 'matters affecting the use' of IP rights *specifically* addressed in the TRIPS Agreement. Aspects of the use of IP rights that are not dealt with in the TRIPS Agreement are not subject to the national treatment or MFN treatment obligations. In addition, unlike the national treatment and MFN treatment obligations of the GATT 1994 and the GATS (see Sections 2.2 to 2.5), the national treatment and MFN treatment obligations of the TRIPS Agreement apply to 'nationals' of other Members rather than to like goods or like services/service suppliers. This is due to the fact that IP rights attach to the IP right holder rather than to the goods or services in which these rights are embodied. The 'nationals' who should be compared are those who seek protection of the same type of IP in comparable situations. Both de jure and de facto discrimination are prohibited.

There are two elements in the test for inconsistency with the national treatment obligation of Article 3.1 of the TRIPS Agreement:

- the measure at issue must relate to the protection of IP covered by the TRIPS Agreement; and
- the nationals of other Members must be accorded 'less favourable' treatment than the nationals of the Member whose measure is challenged.

In *EC – Trademarks and Geographical Indications (2005)*, the United States and Australia challenged an EC regulation that set out procedures for the registration of geographical indications (GIs) for food and agricultural products on the basis of the national treatment obligation of Article 3 of the TRIPS Agreement. The regulation set out additional requirements for the registration of GIs in geographical areas located in third countries outside the European Union. Pursuant to these requirements, which did not apply for the registration of GIs in geographical areas within the European Union, the third country must provide protection to GIs that is both reciprocal and equivalent to that available in the European Union. The panel found that because the regulation dealt with GIs, a category of IP covered by the TRIPS Agreement, the first element of the test for inconsistency with Article 3 was met. With regard to the second element of this test, the panel noted that the European Community regulation distinguished on the basis not of national origin of the IP right holder but of the location of the GIs and thus provided *formally identical* treatment to its own and foreign 'nationals'. However, because the design and structure of the system was such that *in practice* this distinction operated to provide less favourable treatment to foreign nationals with regard to the availability of GI protection, the panel found a violation of Article 3.

Article 4 of the TRIPS Agreement contains the MFN treatment obligation. It requires that any advantage, favour, privilege or immunity with regard to IP protection granted by a Member to the nationals of any other country be accorded immediately and unconditionally to the nationals of all other Members.

For example, it is prohibited for Agricola to require a higher level of originality or artistic creativity to grant copyright protection to works by Alpinian authors and artists than to works by Industrian authors and artists. This would be inconsistent with the MFN treatment obligation of Article 4 of the TRIPS Agreement.

Both the national treatment and the MFN treatment obligations of the TRIPS Agreement are subject to various specific exceptions. For example, Article 5 of the TRIPS Agreement exempts procedures for the acquisition of IP rights provided in multilateral agreements negotiated under the auspices of the WIPO from the national treatment and MFN treatment obligations of Articles 3 and 4.

The TRIPS Agreement further contains transparency obligations in Article 63. WTO Members are required to publish the national laws, regulations, judicial decisions and administrative rulings they adopt that are relevant to IP protection.

The procedural aspects for the acquisition and maintenance of IP rights are addressed in Part IV of the TRIPS Agreement. It allows Members to require compliance with procedures and formalities as a condition for the acquisition or maintenance of IP rights (except copyright and undisclosed information) but limits these to what is 'reasonable'.

Finally, the TRIPS Agreement acknowledges the difficulties least-developed country Members may face in implementing their obligations under this Agreement and their need for flexibility to create a viable technological base. It thus provided a transition period of ten years for implementation of its obligations, aside from those of national treatment and MFN treatment, for these Members (Article 66.1). This transitional period has been extended by the TRIPS Council until 1 January 2033. The TRIPS Agreement also contains commitments on technical cooperation and incentives for transfer of technology (Articles 67 and 66.2).

Note that the TRIPS Agreement does not provide for rules on the issue of 'exhaustion' of IP rights; that is, the question whether the right to control the distribution (such as by resale) of a product embodying an IP right is 'exhausted' world-wide when the holder of this right brings the product to a certain market, or, on the contrary, whether this right is only 'exhausted' on that specific national or regional market. This issue is important because it affects the possibility to legally import and resell a product if it was put on the market of the exporting country with the consent of the IP right holder (known as *parallel importation*). This issue has explicitly been excluded from multilateral rules, and WTO Members are therefore free to determine their own rules on the exhaustion of IP rights.

6.4.3 Specific obligations

Part II of the TRIPS Agreement contains the mandatory minimum standards of protection that Members are obliged to provide in their territories to nationals of other Members in respect of specific IP rights. Note that IP protection confers negative rights; that is, the right to exclude others from the use of the protected subject matter for a particular period of time. It does not confer positive rights, such as the right to produce or market the product embodying the IP right. Each IP right has a different content, depending on the subject matter of its protection. The minimum protection provided in the TRIPS Agreement therefore differs considerably from IP right to IP right. Sections 1 to 7 of Part II provide, with respect to the various categories of IP rights they address, the subject matter that is eligible for protection, the scope of the rights conferred by the relevant category of IP and the permitted exceptions to those rights (discussed in Section 6.4.3).

Examples of minimum standards of protection of specific IP rights, prescribed in Part II of the TRIPS Agreement, are the following:

- Members must protect copyright in literary, scientific and artistic works during the author's entire lifetime and during a period of at least fifty years after his or her death (Articles 9 and 12);
- Members are obliged to grant exclusive rights, renewable indefinitely, to a trademark owner to use the identical or similar mark in the course of trade with respect to identical or similar goods or services, where such use would result in the likelihood of confusion (Articles 16 and 18);
- Members are required to provide interested parties with the legal means to prevent use of any means in the designation or presentation of a good that misleads the public as to the geographical origin of the good (Article 22); and
- Members must provide patent protection, for at least twenty years from the date of filing of the patent, to any

invention in any field, provided that it is new, involves an inventive step and is capable of industrial application (Articles 27 and 33).

In Part II of the TRIPS Agreement, various provisions dealing with different categories of IP rights incorporate specific articles of the relevant WIPO conventions. With regard to the Berne Convention, the Paris Convention and the IPIC Treaty, these provisions oblige all WTO Members, even those that are not parties to the WIPO conventions, to comply with the incorporated articles of these WIPO conventions. In addition, the provisions of Part II of the TRIPS Agreement strengthen and update the protection provided in the relevant WIPO conventions. For instance, copyright protection provided for in the Berne Convention must be extended to computer programmes and compilations of data (Article 10 of the TRIPS Agreement). Similarly, in order to prevent dilution of 'well-known' trademarks, the protection against the use of such trademarks on identical or similar goods provided for in the Paris Convention is extended. It covers also the use of 'well-known' trademarks on goods or services that are *not similar* to those in respect of which a trademark is registered, where such use would 'indicate a connection' between the relevant goods or services and the trademark owner and thereby damage the latter's interests (Article 16 of the TRIPS Agreement). This additional protection aims to address concerns of some WTO Members that the WIPO conventions do not sufficiently meet the needs of certain business sectors in the 'post-industrial era' or 'information age'.

6.4.4 *Exceptions*

There are no general exceptions to the obligations of the TRIPS Agreement comparable to those in Article XX of the GATT 1994 and Article XIV of the GATS (discussed in Sections 4.2 and 4.3). Instead, in addition to the incorporated exceptions of the relevant WIPO conventions, specific provisions allowing Members to grant exceptions from IP protection are provided by the TRIPS Agreement in respect of each of the categories of IP rights covered in Part II (*inter alia*, Article 13 in respect of copyright, Article 17 in respect of trademarks and Article 30 in respect of patents). These exceptions aim to give effect to the balancing objective of the TRIPS Agreement between the need to reward IP right holders for their creations and the public interest in access to the protected matter.

By way of example, Article 13 of the TRIPS Agreement allows Members to provide exceptions to the exclusive rights of a copyright holder if three cumulative requirements are met; namely, the exceptions must:

- be confined to certain special cases;
- not conflict with a normal exploitation of the work; and
- not unreasonably prejudice the legitimate interests of the right holder.

This exception has been interpreted to have a 'narrow or limited operation'.

At issue in *US – Section 110(5) Copyright Act (2000)* were two exemptions in Section 110(5) of the US Copyright Act that allowed the playing of radio and television music in public places such as bars, shops and restaurants without the payment of royalty fees. The 'business exemption' allowed the non-payment of royalties if the size of the establishment was limited to a certain square footage, and the 'homestyle exemption' allowed small restaurants and shops to amplify broadcasts of music using 'homestyle equipment' (i.e. equipment of a kind commonly used in private homes). The United States argued that both exemptions met the conditions of Article 13. The panel emphasized the narrow nature of Article 13. It held that the first condition of Article 13 entails that limitations under Article 13 should be 'clearly defined' and 'narrow in scope and reach' and found that the 'business exemption' did not comply with this condition because the substantial majority of eating and drinking establishments were covered by this exemption, and it therefore did not constitute a 'certain special case'. Furthermore, the panel clarified that, under the second condition of Article 13, the commercial use of a work does not necessarily conflict with its normal exploitation unless the use of a work 'enters into economic competition with the ways the right holders normally extract economic value from that right'. Because the right holders of musical works would expect to be in a position to receive compensation for the use of their works by the establishments covered by the business exemption, the panel found that the second condition was not met. Under the third condition, unreasonable prejudice was found to exist if the exemption 'causes or has the potential to cause an unreasonable loss of income to the copyright owner', which was the case for the business exemption. The panel therefore found the 'business exemption' not to be justified under Article 13 of the TRIPS Agreement. With regard to the 'homestyle exemption', the panel found that all three conditions of Article 13 were fulfilled and that this exemption was therefore lawful.

Also in respect of the 'limited exceptions' allowed under Articles 17 and 30 of the TRIPS Agreement, panels have held that the term 'exceptions' connotes a 'limited derogation, one that does not undercut the body of rules from which it is made' and that the addition of the word 'limited' emphasizes that the exception must be 'narrow and permit only a small diminution of rights'.

Another example is the exception to the rights of a patent holder provided in Article 31 of the TRIPS Agreement, whereby a WTO Member may, under certain conditions, grant a producer a compulsory license to enable the producer to manufacture a product that is protected by a patent and which would thus normally not be able to be produced and traded without the permission of the patent holder. The issue of compulsory licences came to the forefront of public attention with respect to anti-retroviral drugs used in the treatment of HIV/AIDS, on which large pharmaceutical companies have patents and which were marketed by these companies at excessively high prices in developing countries. Compulsory licences could address this problem by allowing domestic producers to use the patent to produce cheaper generic versions of such essential medicines. However, one of the conditions for the granting of compulsory licences, set out in Article 31(f), is that the use of the patent shall be authorized predominantly for the supply of the domestic market of the authorizing Member. Article 31(f) thus prevents Members from granting compulsory licences to produce generic medicines predominantly for export. Consequently, Article 31(f) undermines access to essential medicines by those developing and least-developed countries that have insufficient manufacturing capacity to produce generic medicines themselves under compulsory licences. In 2003, a waiver from Article 31(f) was adopted by the General Council. Subsequently, in order to create a permanent solution to the problem, in 2005, the General Council adopted the decision to amend the TRIPS Agreement by inserting a new Article 31*bis* and a new Annex into the TRIPS Agreement providing that the requirement of Article 31(f) does not apply to the grant by a Member of a compulsory licence necessary for the production of a pharmaceutical product and its export to an 'eligible' importing Member in accordance with the terms set out in paragraph 2 of the new Annex to the TRIPS Agreement. This amendment will take effect as soon as it is ratified by two-thirds of WTO Members.

6.4.5 *Enforcement of IP rights*

The protection of IP depends not only on substantive rules providing minimum standards of protection, but also on procedural mechanisms providing an effective means to enforce these rules. The TRIPS Agreement is unique (and differs from the existing WIPO conventions) because of the fact that it imposes specific obligations on WTO Members for the effective enforcement of IP rights.

The TRIPS Agreement requires WTO Members to ensure the availability of enforcement procedures set out in Part III 'so as to permit effective action' against infringements of IP rights covered in the TRIPS Agreement, including by providing expeditious remedies to prevent infringements and remedies to deter further infringements (Article 41).

In particular, Members are required to provide civil judicial procedures for the enforcement of any IP right covered by the TRIPS Agreement (Article 42). Criminal procedures and penalties must be available at least in cases of willful trademark counterfeiting or copyright piracy on a commercial scale (Article 61).

These enforcement procedures are subject to due process obligations. WTO Members are not required to provide a separate judicial system for the enforcement of IP rights but may make use of already existing enforcement procedures if these are sufficient to provide the required level of enforcement specified in the TRIPS Agreement.

Furthermore, the TRIPS Agreement deals with provisional measures and border measures to prevent IP infringements. Article 50 of the TRIPS Agreement requires judicial authorities to have the power to order 'prompt and effective provisional measures' to prevent the introduction into commerce of goods embodying an IP infringement once such goods have cleared customs and to preserve evidence relating to such infringements. Article 51, by contrast, addresses border measures applied *before* the relevant goods have cleared customs. In particular, it requires Members to have procedures in place to allow an IP right holder that has valid grounds for suspecting that importation of counterfeit trademark or pirated copyright goods may take place to apply to the competent authorities for the suspension by customs authorities of the release of imported goods in order to prevent IP infringements. Such procedures may also be made available for other IP infringements.

6.4.6 Institutional and procedural provisions

Article 68 of the TRIPS Agreement establishes the TRIPS Council, composed of all WTO Members. The TRIPS Council provides a forum for Members to consult on all matters pertaining to the TRIPS Agreement. It also monitors the operation of the TRIPS Agreement and Members' compliance with their obligations thereunder.

Pursuant to Article 64.1, disputes under the TRIPS Agreement are subject to the system for dispute settlement of the WTO (discussed in Chapter 8). This represents an important achievement of the TRIPS Agreement because prior to the TRIPS Agreement disputes on international rules regarding IP rights were not subject to an effective dispute settlement system.

The TRIPS Agreement contains one special dispute settlement rule with regard to the possible causes of action that deviates from normal WTO dispute settlement rules. Although normally Members can bring violation, non-violation and situation complaints (discussed in Section 8.4), for a period of five years from the entry into force of the WTO Agreement, no non-violation or situation complaints could be brought under the TRIPS Agreement (Article 64.2). This moratorium has been extended a number of times and currently still applies while Members continue the examination of the modalities for such complaints.

Further reading

TBT Agreement

Broude, T., and Levy, P. I. (2014) 'Do you mind if I do not smoke? Products, purpose and indeterminacy in US – Measures Affecting the Production and Sale of Clove Cigarettes', *World Trade Review* 13 (2) 357–392.

Marceau, G. (2014) 'A comment on the Appellate Body Report in EC-Seal Products in the context of the trade and environment debate', *Review of European, Comparative & International Environmental Law* 23(3) 318–328.

Philip, I. L., and Donald, H. R. (2015) 'EC–Seal Products: seals and sensibilities (TBT aspects of the panel and Appellate Body reports)', *World Trade Review* 14(2) 337–379.

Wijkström, E., and McDaniels, D. (2013) 'Improving regulatory governance: international standards and the WTO TBT Agreement', *Journal of World Trade* 47(5) 1013–1046.

SPS Agreement

Foster, E. C. (2008) 'Public opinion and the interpretation of the World Trade Organization's Agreement on Sanitary and Phytosanitary Measures', *Journal of International Economic Law* 11(2) 427–458.

Mercurio, B., and Shao, D. (2010) 'A precautionary approach to decision making: the evolving jurisprudence on Article 5.7 of the SPS Agreement', *Trade Law and Development* 2(2) 195–223.

Wouters, J., and Geraets, D. (2012) 'Private food standards and the World Trade Organization: some legal considerations' *World Trade Review* 11 479–489.

TRIPS Agreement

Frankel, S. (2009) 'Some consequences of misinterpreting the TRIPS Agreement', *The W.I.P.O. Journal* 1(1) 35–42.

Slade, A. (2014) 'Good faith and the TRIPS Agreement: putting flesh on the bones of the TRIPS "objectives"', *International And Comparative Law Quarterly* 63(2) 353–383.

Yu, P. K. (2009) 'The global intellectual property order and its undetermined future', *The W.I.P.O. Journal* 1(1) 1–15.

Chapter 7

The institutional aspects of the WTO

7.1 Introduction

The World Trade Organization (WTO) was established under the WTO Agreement and became operational on 1 January 1995. The WTO Agreement was signed on 15 April 1994 in Marrakesh, Morocco, by the countries and customs territories that had participated in the Uruguay Round of multilateral trade negotiations (hereinafter the Uruguay Round) from 1986 to 1993. The establishment of the WTO is seen by many as the most important result of the Uruguay Round. Although the WTO is the youngest of the major international intergovernmental organizations, it is arguably among the most influential international organizations in these times of economic globalization.

The origins of the WTO lie in the General Agreement on Tariffs and Trade of 1947 (GATT 1947), which had functioned for almost fifty years as a de facto international organization for trade. At the end of the 1940s, the international community had not succeeded in establishing an international organization for trade alongside the newly created international economic organizations, namely the World Bank and the International Monetary Fund (IMF). Although the Havana Charter establishing an 'International Trade Organization' was concluded in 1948, it never came into force because of the refusal of the US Congress to approve this agreement. The GATT 1947, which was conceived as a multilateral agreement for the reduction of tariffs and other barriers to trade, and not as an international organization, gradually and very pragmatically, took on the central tasks of the 'stillborn' International Trade Organization. The decisions, procedures and customary practices of the GATT 1947 still guide the WTO (Article XVI:1 of the WTO Agreement).

The GATT 1947 had much success with regard to the reduction of customs duties, particularly on industrial products. However, it was less successful in reducing non-tariff barriers to trade. During the Uruguay Round, the conviction gradually grew that the international community needed a fully fledged international organization to efficiently guide and regulate the increasingly complex trade relations between countries. This conviction, championed by Canada, the European Union (EU), and Mexico but not by the United States, finally led to the establishment of the WTO.

7.2 Objectives

Pursuant to the Preamble of the WTO Agreement, the ultimate objectives of the WTO are:

- the increase of standards of living;
- the attainment of full employment;
- the growth of real income and effective demand; and
- the expansion of production of and trade in goods and services.

However, it is clear from the Preamble that, in pursuing these objectives, the WTO must take into account the objective of sustainable development and the needs of developing countries. These preambular statements contradict the contention that the WTO is only about trade liberalization without regard for the sustainability of economic development, environmental degradation and global poverty. The WTO agreements must be read in the light of the objectives set out in the Preamble.

In *US – Shrimp (1998)*, the Appellate Body stated: '[The language of the Preamble to the WTO Agreement] demonstrates a recognition by WTO negotiators that optimal use of the world's resources should be made in accordance with the objective of sustainable development. As this preambular language reflects the intentions of negotiators of the WTO Agreement, we believe it must add colour, texture and shading to our interpretation of the agreements annexed to the WTO Agreement, in this case, the GATT 1994'.

7.3 Functions

The primary function of the WTO is to provide the common institutional framework for the conduct of trade relations among its Members. More specifically, the WTO, as set out in Article III (and Article V) of the WTO Agreement, has been assigned the following broad functions:

- to facilitate the implementation, administration and operation of the WTO agreements, as well as to further the
  objectives of these agreements;
- to be a forum for the negotiation of new trade rules;
- to settle trade disputes between its Members (see Chapter 8);
- to review the trade policies of its Members; and
- to cooperate with other international organizations and
  non-governmental organizations.

In addition, although not explicitly mentioned in the WTO
Agreement, the WTO undisputedly has the function of
giving technical assistance to developing-country Members.
Each of these functions is discussed briefly next.

7.3.1 Facilitation of the implementation of the WTO agreements

The function of facilitating the implementation, administration and operation of the WTO agreements and
furthering their objectives is an essential function of the
WTO. It involves most of its bodies and takes up much
of their time.

An example of what this function of 'facilitating' implementation entails is found in Article 12.2 of the SPS
Agreement, pursuant to which the SPS Committee has
created a mechanism whereby Members may raise at
each regular meeting of the SPS Committee the specific

> trade concerns they have with regard to other Members'
> sanitary or phytosanitary measures. The multilateral dis-
> cussion of these concerns may lead (and frequently does
> lead) to revision of the relevant measure or to the provi-
> sion of technical assistance to comply with the measure.
> In this way, trade concerns can be addressed without
> recourse to dispute settlement.

7.3.2 Negotiations

A second function of the WTO is to provide a forum for
negotiations among WTO Members on new trade rules.
Before the WTO was established, multilateral trade negotiations were conducted in specially convened, time-limited
rounds of negotiations, covering a wide variety of issues.
The WTO now provides for a permanent forum for negotiations among its Members, in which each trade issue can be
negotiated separately on its own merits.

> Examples of trade agreements negotiated in the framework
> of the WTO include the amendment of the provisions of
> the TRIPS Agreement regarding compulsory licensing, to
> ensure access to essential medicines; the amendment of the
> Agreement on Government Procurement to extend its
> coverage; the accession of thirty-three countries to the
> WTO; and the adoption of the Information Technology
> Agreement.

Although it was initially thought that specially con-vened rounds of negotiations would no longer be necessary, it soon became apparent that, for multilateral negotiations on trade liberalization to be successful, the political momen-tum and opportunity for package deals brought by old GATT-style negotiation rounds is needed. Members there-fore agreed at the Doha Ministerial Conference of 2001 to launch a new round of multilateral trade negotiations, com-monly known as the 'Doha Round', with an ambitious agenda. The Doha Round initially adopted a 'single under-taking' approach, meaning that there is no agreement on anything until there is agreement on everything. However, in view of several missed deadlines and repeated deadlocks in the negotiations on core issues, Members decided to abandon the 'single undertaking' approach and advance negotiations in areas where progress was possible. At the Bali Ministerial Conference in December 2013, twelve years after the start of the Doha Round, agreement was reached on a limited number of issues on the negotiating agenda, including trade facilitation, public stockholding for food security purposes and issues relating to preferential treat-ment of least-developed countries (LDCs). Subsequently, in November 2014, WTO Members adopted the Agreement on Trade Facilitation, to be inserted into the WTO Agreement and to enter into force once two-thirds of Members have completed their domestic ratification process. On the many remaining issues on the agenda of the Doha Round, and in particular on non-agricultural market access (NAMA), trade in agricultural products and trade in services, the negotia-tions continue.

7.3.3 Dispute settlement

A third and very important function of the WTO is the administration of the WTO dispute settlement system. The prompt settlement of disputes under the WTO agreements is essential for the effective functioning of the WTO and for maintaining a proper balance between the rights and obligations of Members (Article 3.2 of the DSU). Chapter 8 examines the basic principles, institutions and procedures of the WTO dispute settlement system.

7.3.4 Trade policy review

A fourth function of the WTO is to administer the WTO Trade Policy Review Mechanism (TPRM). Under the TPRM, the trade policies and practices of all WTO Members are subject to periodic review by the Trade Policy Review Body (TPRB) (see Section 7.4) on the basis of a report by the Member under review and a report by the WTO Secretariat. These reports, together with the minutes of the meeting of the TPRB and the concluding remarks by the TPRB Chair are published shortly after the review. The TPRM aims to achieve greater transparency with regard to the trade policies and practices of Members and to contribute to improved compliance by Members with their WTO obligations. The TPRM may serve to 'shame' a Member into complying with its WTO obligations or publicly support its WTO-consistent (but domestically contested) policies. Trade policy review reports can be found on the WTO website and are a very useful source of information on the trade policies and practices of WTO Members.

7.3.5 *Cooperation with other organizations*

A fifth function of the WTO is cooperation with other organizations. Article III:5 of the WTO Agreement requires the WTO to cooperate with the IMF and the World Bank in order to ensure coherence in global economic policy. The WTO has given effect to this obligation through concluding cooperation agreements with the IMF and the World Bank. The WTO is also required to cooperate with other international organizations that have responsibilities related to those of the WTO (Article V:1 of the WTO Agreement). The WTO has made arrangements for cooperation with many international organizations, including United Nations Conference on Trade and Development (UNCTAD), World Intellectual Property Organization (WIPO) and the World Health Organization (WHO). About 140 international organizations have observer status with WTO councils or committees, and the WTO likewise participates in the work of many international organizations.

Furthermore, as allowed by Article V:2 of the WTO Agreement, the General Council has made appropriate arrangements for consultation and cooperation with non-governmental organizations (NGOs). Although NGOs have no role in WTO decision-making, a significant improvement in the relationship between the WTO and civil society has been achieved through pragmatic initiatives by the WTO Secretariat, including regular briefings for NGOs on the work of the WTO, symposia and public fora, dissemination of NGO position papers to WTO Members and the general public, the setting up of an NGO centre at ministerial conferences and improved access to WTO documents through faster derestriction.

7.3.6 Technical assistance to developing countries

A sixth function of the WTO is the provision of technical assistance to developing-country Members to allow them to integrate into the world trading system and to reap the benefits of international trade. Although this task is not explicitly stated in the WTO Agreement, its importance is emphasized in the Doha Ministerial Declaration of December 2001.

> In paragraph 38 of the Doha Ministerial Declaration of 2001, WTO Members stated, 'We confirm that technical cooperation and capacity building are core elements of the development dimension of the multilateral trading system ... We instruct the Secretariat, in coordination with other relevant agencies, to support domestic efforts for mainstreaming trade into national plans for economic development and strategies for poverty reduction'.

Several WTO agreements provide for technical assistance to developing-country Members by other Members or by the WTO. Technical assistance provided by the WTO is funded mainly from the Doha Development Agenda Global Trust Fund, to which Members make voluntary contributions. These activities include e-learning courses, regional trade policy courses, advanced trade policy courses held in Geneva, the 'WTO reference centres' in developing countries, the 'Geneva Week' to update developing-country Members with no permanent representation in Geneva on recent developments at the WTO, technical support missions to specific developing-country Members, and support for research and teaching in developing-country Members on WTO law and international trade. At the Hong Kong Ministerial Conference in December 2005, the WTO launched the Aid for Trade Initiative to mobilize resources to address the trade-related capacity constraints faced by developing and least-developed countries and coordinate the aid for trade given by national, regional and international donors and organizations.

7.4 Institutional structure

The WTO has a complex institutional structure with numerous permanent and temporary bodies to carry out its tasks (Article IV of the WTO Agreement). This institutional structure is illustrated in Figure 7.1.

At the highest level is the Ministerial Conference (Article IV:1 of the WTO Agreement). The Ministerial Conference consists of representatives at ministerial level of all WTO Members. It is in session for only a few days every two years. The Ministerial Conference is competent to make decisions on *all* WTO matters. It has further explicitly been granted specific powers, including adopting authoritative interpretations of the WTO agreements, granting waivers of WTO obligations, adopting amendments to the WTO

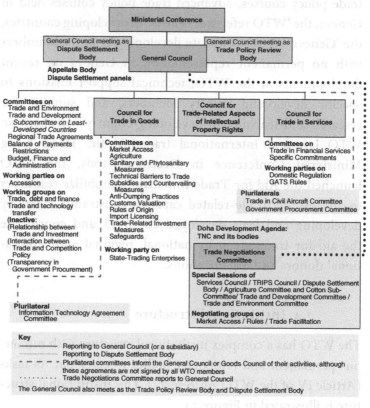

Figure 7.1: WTO Structure (source: WTO website)

agreements, making decisions on accession to the WTO, appointing the WTO Director-General and adopting staff regulations.

At the second level, there is the General Council (Article IV:2 of the WTO Agreement). The General Council exercises all the powers of the Ministerial Conference in between its sessions. It consists of ambassador-level diplomats of all WTO Members. The General Council normally meets every two months in Geneva. The General Council has two alter egos, namely, the Dispute Settlement Body (DSB) and the Trade Policy Review Body (TPRB). When the General Council convenes to discharge its responsibilities relating to dispute settlement (see Chapter 8), it convenes as the DSB, which has its own chairperson and its own procedural rules. When the General Council convenes to discharge its responsibilities relating to the review of a WTO Member's trade policies (see Section 7.3.4), it convenes as the TPRB, which also has its own chairperson and procedural rules. The DSB and the TPRB meet more frequently than does the General Council.

The Ministerial Conference and the General Council are supported by the Council for Trade in Goods (CTG), the Council for Trade in Services (CTS) and the Council for Trade-Related Aspects of Intellectual Property Rights (TRIPS Council) (Article IV:5 of the WTO Agreement). These specialized Councils, on which all WTO Members are represented, are responsible for overseeing the functioning of the multilateral agreements on trade in goods, the GATS and the TRIPS Agreement, respectively. They meet as often as necessary.

The institutional structure of the WTO further comprises around thirty-five permanent and thirty ad hoc bodies. The permanent bodies include the Committee on Trade and Development, the Committee on Regional Trade Agreements and the Committee on Trade and Environment. In addition, all but one of the multilateral agreements on trade in goods establish a committee to carry out functions relating to the implementation of the relevant agreement, for example the Committee on Technical Barriers to Trade (TBT Committee) (see Section 6.2.3) and the Committee on Subsidies and Countervailing Measures. The ad hoc bodies are mainly Working Groups on accession and negotiating bodies established especially for the Doha Round negotiations. The Doha Round negotiations are supervised by the temporarily established Trade Negotiations Committee (TNC), which reports to the General Council.

Every year, there are hundreds of meetings of WTO councils, committees and working parties that take place at the WTO headquarters in Geneva. It is nearly impossible for developing countries with no or a limited diplomatic representation in Geneva to attend all the meetings in which issues of importance to them are discussed. Furthermore, the often very technical and/or complex legal nature of the trade issues discussed at WTO meetings creates significant challenges for Members' representatives to the WTO.

Unlike other international organizations with a large membership, the WTO does not have an executive body composed of a limited number of representative WTO Members to facilitate the process of negotiation and decision-making. Instead, all WTO bodies are composed of representatives of all 162 WTO Members, making negotiations in these bodies very difficult and time-consuming. Furthermore, the WTO does not have a permanent body through which the 'dialogue' between the WTO and civil society representatives, such as national parliamentarians, employee and employer organizations, environmental organizations and human rights organizations, can take place.

The institutional structure of the WTO also includes non-political, independent, judicial or quasi-judicial bodies and, in particular, the ad hoc dispute settlement panels and the permanent Appellate Body (see Section 8.5).

The WTO is serviced by its Secretariat based in Geneva, which is responsible for the smooth functioning of the organization. Its main tasks are to provide technical and professional support to the various WTO bodies, to provide technical assistance to developing countries, to monitor and analyze developments in world trade, to provide information to the public and the media, to advise governments of countries wishing to become Members of the WTO and to provide administrative and legal assistance to dispute settlement panels. Note that the Appellate Body has its own Secretariat, separate from the WTO Secretariat.

The Secretariat is headed by the WTO Director-General, who is appointed by the Ministerial Conference. The appointment of a new Director-General is typically a contentious process. New procedures were adopted in 2009 to facilitate the appointment process. The current WTO Director-General is Roberto Azevêdo, previously Ambassador of Brazil to the WTO and other international economic organizations in Geneva.

The WTO Secretariat staff and the Director-General are independent and impartial international officials. They may not seek or accept instructions from any government or any authority external to the WTO (Article VI:4 of the WTO Agreement).

WTO Members often emphasize that the WTO is 'a Member-driven' organization. The Members – and not the

Director-General or the WTO Secretariat – set the agenda, make proposals and take decisions. The Director-General and the WTO Secretariat have no autonomous policy decision-making powers. They act mainly as an 'honest broker' in or a 'facilitator' of the political decision-making processes in the WTO.

The WTO Secretariat is of limited size (less than 650 regular staff as compared to 12,335 regular staff of the World Bank) and possesses limited financial resources (a budget of about US$ 195 million in 2014, as compared to the World Bank's administrative budget of US$2.6 billion in the same year). Nevertheless, a WTO Director-General with vision and drive can play an important role by building consensus among WTO Members on particular agreements or decisions.

7.5 Membership

Since the accession of the People's Republic of China in December 2001, the WTO can be regarded as a universal organization. Its 162 Members account for 99.5 per cent of the world's population and about 98 per cent of all international trade.

This section will examine the current membership of the WTO, the accession process and the obligations and rights of membership.

7.5.1 Current membership

As stated, the WTO has 162 Members at present (i.e. as of 1 December 2015). This membership is very diverse.

Three-quarters of WTO Members are developing countries. There is no WTO definition of a 'developing country'. Instead, developing-country status is largely based on self-selection by Members. Developing countries may rely on the special and differential treatment provisions in various WTO agreements and may receive technical assistance. One-fifth of WTO Members are least-developed countries (LDCs). The WTO recognizes as LDCs those countries that have been classified as such by the United Nations. Additional special and differential treatment is provided for in WTO agreements for LDC Members.

It is noteworthy that not only States but also separate customs territories with full autonomy in the conduct of their external commercial relations – such as Hong Kong, China; Macau, China; and Chinese Taipei – can be, and are, Members of the WTO. Equally noteworthy is that both the European Union (before 2010 referred to as the European Communities) and all twenty-eight Member States of the European Union are Members of the WTO (Article XI:1 of the WTO Agreement). In practice, it is the European Commission that speaks and acts for the European Union and all its Member States in WTO matters (except in the Budget Committee).

WTO Members organize themselves, formally and informally, into various groups and alliances around common interests or positions. For example, previously, the Cairns Group of nineteen agriculture-exporting countries and currently the G-20 group of developing countries have been influential in the negotiations for the liberalization of agricultural trade. Other coalitions include the G-90 group

247

representing the interests of the poorest Members and the 'Cotton-Four' group of West African countries that campaign against the policies of the European Union and United States that distort trade in cotton. Groups of WTO Members have also emerged to allow negotiations in smaller groups, to permit compromises to be reached or to break deadlocks. Previously the 'Quad', composed of the United States, the European Communities, Canada and Japan, was at the core of all negotiations. Currently, reflecting the new geopolitical reality and the growing economic importance of certain developing-country Members, the Quad has been replaced by the G-5, consisting of the United States, the European Union, China, Brazil and India. Without agreement among these key Members, no progress can be made in WTO nego-tiations. Furthermore, in recent years, a large group of devel-oping countries, including Argentina, Venezuela, Chile, Peru, Mexico, Thailand, the Philippines, Indonesia, Malaysia, Turkey and Pakistan, often acting as part of a coalition or alliance, has gained significantly in influence in WTO decision-making and negotiations. The WTO is clearly no longer the 'rich man's club' it was in its early days.

7.5.2 Accession

The WTO Agreement initially provided for two ways to become a WTO Member. First, Contracting Parties to the GATT 1947 could become 'original' Members of the WTO by accepting the terms of the WTO Agreement and the multi-lateral trade agreements and by making concessions and commitments for trade in goods and trade in services, respectively (Article XI:1 of the WTO Agreement). This method was only available at the time of and shortly after the establishment of the WTO.

Second, a state or separate customs territory can negotiate accession to the WTO by accepting the terms of the WTO Agreement and the multilateral trade agreements and negotiating the terms of accession with the current WTO Members (Article XII of the WTO Agreement). This way of becoming a Member is open indefinitely.

Accession to the WTO is typically a long and difficult process.

China's accession negotiations lasted fifteen years and those of Russia eighteen years. The shortest accession process has been that of Kyrgyzstan, lasting two years and eleven months.

There are four main phases in the accession process. First, the applicant state or customs territory has to submit a report or 'memorandum' on its trade and economic policies. A working party of all interested WTO Members is established to examine, on the basis of this report and other information, the WTO-consistency of the applicant's laws, regulations and administrative procedures.

Second, candidates for membership must bring their national laws, regulations and administrative procedures into conformity with their obligations under the WTO agreements. Current WTO Members will often have very specific concerns and demands in this respect and will carefully monitor whether these concerns and demands are addressed. Candidates for membership also have to negotiate a 'ticket of admission' in the form of market access concessions. When they join the WTO, new Members immediately benefit from all the gains in market access achieved by existing WTO Members. In return, they must 'pay' for this benefit by offering access to their own markets to WTO Members. The 'price' of this ticket of admission depends on the level of economic development of the acceding country and is the subject of the accession negotiations. Since different WTO Members have different trade interests, these negotiations are necessarily bilateral. However, the outcome of these negotiations is 'multilateralized' (i.e. it applies equally to all WTO Members) due to the most-favoured-nation (MFN) treatment obligation (see Sections 2.2 and 2.3).

The third stage of the accession process entails the drafting of the 'terms of membership' in the working party report, the draft Protocol of Accession and the draft Goods and Services Schedules of the candidate, containing its market access concessions and commitments. It is possible that, to secure accession to the WTO, a candidate for membership must accept additional ('WTO-plus') obligations or limited ('WTO-minus') rights. This will be reflected in the Protocol of Accession.

For example, China undertook the 'WTO-plus' obligation to eliminate export duties on all its products, except those listed in Annex 6 to its Protocol of Accession (paragraph 11.3 of the Protocol of Accession of China), whereas most other WTO Members are not subject to such an obligation. In addition, China had to agree to WTO-minus rights in the form of a twelve-year transitional product-specific safeguard mechanism, under which other WTO Members could, more easily than under the normal rules on safeguards, restrict Chinese exports that caused or threatened to cause market disruption (paragraph 16 of the Protocol of Accession of China).

The final stage of the accession process is the 'decision stage', in which the General Council or the Ministerial Conference decides on the application for membership. If the application is approved, the candidate becomes a WTO Member thirty days after it has deposited the instrument of ratification of its Protocol of Accession.

To date, thirty-three accessions have been successfully completed. At this moment, twenty-one countries are negotiating their accession to the WTO.

7.5.3 *Membership obligations and rights*

Article XVI:4 of the WTO Agreement requires every Member to ensure that its laws, regulations and administrative procedures comply with the obligations of the WTO agreements. However, in exceptional circumstances in which it is very difficult or impossible for a Member to comply with its obligations, it may be granted a time-limited waiver from specific obligations by the Ministerial Conference or the General Council (Article IX:3 of the WTO Agreement).

There are several well-known examples of waivers granted to WTO Members. These include the waiver from the obligations under Articles I, IX and XIII of the GATT 1994 that was granted to a group of Members allowing them to ban trade in 'blood diamonds' (i.e. diamonds sold to fund conflicts in Africa) under the Kimberly Process. Another notable example is the waiver from the obligations of Article 31(f) and (h) of the TRIPS Agreement granted to WTO Members that produce essential medicines, under compulsory licences, for export to those Members that lack sufficient domestic capacity to manufacture these medicines themselves.

In addition to the possibility to be granted a waiver from certain WTO obligations, WTO law also provides the possibility for a Member to 'opt out' of the application of WTO rules with respect to another Member (Article XIII of the WTO Agreement) for political, economic or other reasons. The non-application clause may only be invoked at the time either of the two Members involved becomes a WTO Member and no later. The decision to 'opt out' must be notified to the General Council or Ministerial Conference before it takes a decision on the accession of the Member involved. The 'opt-out' possibility has been of limited practical importance to date.

The non-application clause has been invoked only eleven times to date. Seven of these were 'opt outs' by the United States with regard to former communist countries acceding to the WTO. Most recently, in 2011, the United States invoked the non-application clause when the Russian Federation was acceding to the WTO. In response, Russia did likewise. These opt-outs have all been revoked. In addition, Turkey invoked the non-application clause with regard to Armenia, and El Salvador did so with regard to China. The latter two 'opt-outs' are the only ones currently still in force.

In recognition of the particular difficulties that developing-country Members may face in participating in international trade, most WTO agreements provide for special and differential treatment (S&D treatment) of these Members. These S&D treatment provisions include those that (1) grant transitional periods to developing-country Members to comply with certain WTO obligations, (2) allow greater flexibility to developing-country Members in making commitments or using policy instruments, (3) encourage the granting of technical assistance to developing-country Members, (4) aim at increasing the trade opportunities for developing-country Members and (5) provide that developed Members should safeguard the interests of developing-country Members. However, because most S&D treatment provisions are either couched in hortatory terms or contain only 'best-endeavour' obligations, they are not easily enforceable.

An example of a S&D treatment obligation of 'best-endeavour' is that at issue in the *EC – Approval and Marketing of Biotech Products (2006)* dispute. In this dispute, Argentina relied on the S&D treatment provision contained in Article 10.1 of the SPS Agreement, which provides that, in the preparation and application of SPS measures, 'Members shall take account of the needs of developing country Members'. Argentina argued that the European Union had not taken account of the great economic impact of its restrictions on importation and sale of biotech products on Argentina. This impact was due to Argentina's status as the world's largest developing-country producer of biotech products and its economic dependence on agricultural exports. The panel, however, held that the obligation 'to take account' of developing-country needs entails only the obligation 'to consider' these needs and does not prescribe any result to be achieved.

With one exception of minor importance, the WTO Agreement does not provide for the possibility to expel Members from the WTO. There is no procedure to expel even Members that systematically violate their WTO obligations or that are guilty of gross violations of human rights or acts of aggression.

Members can unilaterally withdraw from the WTO under Article XV:1 of the WTO Agreement. Withdrawal applies to all the multilateral trade agreements – it is not possible to withdraw from certain of these agreements and not others. The withdrawal takes effect six months after the notification of the decision to withdraw has been received by the WTO Director-General. No Member has made use of the withdrawal possibility to date.

7.6 Decision-making procedures

In terms of Article IX:1 of the WTO Agreement, WTO Members must first try to take decisions by consensus. A decision is considered to be taken by consensus if no Member present at the meeting when the decision is taken *formally* objects to the proposed decision. In other words, an express objection is needed to prevent a decision being taken. No voting occurs. Each Member has veto power, but Members generally refrain from blocking a consensus unless significant national interests are at stake. A certain degree of deference to economic power occurs.

In theory, when a decision cannot be taken by consensus, it may be taken by majority voting. The required majority varies with the subject matter of the decision. In general, a simple majority is sufficient for a decision to be adopted. However, certain special decision-making procedures are provided for in respect of particular decisions.

For example, a three-fourths majority of the Members is required to adopt an authoritative interpretation of a WTO agreement and to adopt a waiver of WTO obligations (Article IX:3 of the WTO Agreement). For decisions on accession, a two-thirds majority of the Members is required (Article XII:2 of the WTO Agreement).

Each WTO Member has one vote, except for the European Union, which has as many votes as it has Member States (currently twenty-eight). When the European Union exercises its voting right, the European Union Member States, which are all full Members of the WTO (see Section 7.5.1), may not participate in the voting. In practice, however, this matters little, because the WTO very seldom resorts to voting. WTO decisions are made almost exclusively by consensus.

Although the consensus requirement renders decision-making by the WTO difficult and susceptible to paralysis, decision-making by consensus is at the heart of the WTO system and is regarded as a fundamental democratic guarantee. It is also a guarantee of the presence of sufficient economic and political support for the decision to ensure its implementation.

In the early years of the WTO, developing-country Members objected to their marginalization in WTO negotiations and decision-making. As noted earlier, at present, progress can no longer be made in WTO negotiations without the agreement of China, India and Brazil, all members of the G-5. More generally, whereas many other developing-country Members still lack the resources and expertise to participate effectively in WTO negotiations and decision-making, they have increasingly been able to make their voices heard and their concerns considered in WTO negotiations and decision-making. To large extent, this has been the result of the systematic coordination of positions and the pooling of resources and expertise in groups, coalitions and alliances of developing-country Members with common interests. This welcome development does, however, also have a drawback.

The active and effective participation in WTO negotiations and decision-making of a larger number of developing-country Members with very different economic and trade interests has made it more difficult than ever before to reach consensus.

7.7 Status and budget

The WTO has legal personality and must be granted by its Members the legal capacity, privileges and immunities needed to carry out its functions (Article VIII of the WTO Agreement). The WTO is not part of the UN 'family', but is a fully independent organization. However, it maintains a close working relationship with several UN agencies and bodies (see Section 7.3.5).

The WTO has a rather modest budget compared to other international organizations. In 2014, its total budget amounted to 197 million Swiss Francs. The Financial Regulations, adopted by the General Council, provide that the contribution of each WTO Member to the WTO budget is established on the basis of that Member's international trade (both imports and exports) in relation to the total trade of all Members. Thus, contributions depend on each Member's share in global trade. With respect to Members of which the share in international trade is less than 0.015 per cent, a minimum contribution of 0.015 per cent to the WTO budget is required. The largest contributors to the WTO budget are the Member States of the European Union because their share is calculated taking into account both intra-European Union trade and trade between the European Union and third countries. The European Union itself does not contribute to the WTO budget.

Further reading

Delimatsis, P. (2014) 'Transparency in the WTO's decision-making', *Leiden Journal of International Law* 27 701–726.

Hannah, N. E. (2014) 'The quest for accountable governance: embedded NGOs and demand driven advocacy in the international trade regime', *Journal of World Trade* 48(3) 457–480.

Ghosh, A. (2010) 'Developing countries in the WTO Trade Policy Review Mechanism', *World Trade Review* 9 419–455.

Toohey, L. (2014) 'Accession as dialogue: epistemic communities and the World Trade Organization', *Leiden Journal of International Law* 27 397–418.

Wolfe, R. (2015) 'First diagnose, then treat: what ails the Doha Round'? *World Trade Review* 14 7–28.

World Trade Organization (2014) *World Trade Report 2014: Trade and development: recent trends and the role of the WTO* World Trade Organization, available at: www.wto.org/english/res_e/book sp_e/world_trade_report14_e.pdf

Yamaoka, T. (2013) 'Analysis of China's accession commitments in the WTO: new taxonomy of more and less stringent commitments, and the struggle for mitigation by China', *Journal of World Trade* 47(1) 105–158.

Chapter 8

The WTO dispute settlement system

8.1 Introduction

The WTO possesses a system for the settlement of disputes between its Members that is in many respects unique and quite successful. This system is provided for in the WTO Dispute Settlement Understanding (DSU). It creates a single, integrated system for the resolution of disputes arising under any of the WTO 'covered agreements'.

The WTO dispute settlement system is the most prolific international State-to-State dispute settlement system. From the WTO's establishment in 1995 to date (i.e. 1 December 2015), 500 disputes have been brought to the WTO dispute settlement system, and 194 panel reports and 120 Appellate Body reports have been adopted. Although many of these disputes are of a technical nature, others are politically sensitive and have received extensive media attention.

Disputes that have received much attention from the media include those involving domestic health or environmental legislation: among others, *EC – Approval and Marketing of Biotech Products (2006)*, a dispute on the European approval regime for biotech products; *Brazil – Retreaded Tyres (2007)*, a dispute on Brazilian measures to reduce risks arising from the accumulation of waste tyres; *EC – Hormones (1998)*, a dispute on the European ban on meat from cattle treated with growth hormones; *US – Shrimp (1998)*, a dispute on the US ban on shrimp caught in nets that lead to incidental killing of sea turtles; *US – Tuna II (Mexico) (2012)*, a dispute concerning US requirements for the use of its 'dolphin-safe' label on tinned tuna; *US – Clove Cigarettes (2012)*, a dispute on the US ban on flavoured cigarettes, except menthol cigarettes; and the *China – Raw Materials (2012)* and *China – Rare Earths (2014)* disputes regarding China's export restrictions on natural resources essential in the production of high-technology products. In addition, the *EC and Certain Member States – Large Civil Aircraft (2011)* and *US – Large Civil Aircraft (2012)* disputes, dealing with many billions of euros and dollars of European and American subsidies to Airbus and Boeing, respectively, have been economically very significant and of high political sensitivity. Also much discussed were *EC – Bananas III (1997)*, a dispute on the EU's preferential import regime for bananas from former colonies in Africa, the Caribbean and the Pacific and *EC – Seal Products (2014)*, a dispute on a ban imposed by the European Union on the importation and marketing of seal products, for reasons of public morals.

To date developed-country Members, and in particular the United States and the European Union, have been the most active complainants in the WTO dispute settlement system. However, developing-country Members have frequently used the system to resolve their trade disputes with both other developing-country Members and developed-country Members. Also, whereas the United States and the European Union have been the most active complainants, they are also the Members against whom by far the most cases have been brought.

> Examples of 'David versus Goliath' disputes, include *US - Gambling (2005)*, a challenge by tiny Antigua and Barbuda (an island State with 90 000 inhabitants) against the United States' prohibition of internet gambling and *US - Underwear (1997)*, in which Costa Rica complained against US measures restricting textile imports from Costa Rica.

The WTO dispute settlement system is not entirely novel. It is based on almost fifty years of experience in the resolution of trade disputes in the context of the GATT 1947. The GATT dispute settlement system, which had pragmatically developed on the basis of Articles XXII and XXIII of the GATT 1947, was initially quite successful when GATT dispute settlement was still more diplomatic in nature. However, it also had a number of shortcomings, which became ever more acute as GATT dispute settlement slowly became more judicial in nature. The primary shortcoming of the GATT dispute settlement system was that important decisions, such as those on the establishment of a panel of experts to hear a dispute and on the adoption of the findings and conclusions of panels in order to make them binding, had to be taken by consensus among all GATT contracting parties. This meant that a responding party could prevent the establishment of a panel to hear a case against it or could prevent any conclusions unfavourable to it from becoming binding. In the 1980s, the consensus decision-making requirement of the GATT dispute settlement system made this system largely ineffective. As a result, the United States increasingly turned to unilateral action against what it considered to be violations of GATT law, leading to concerns by other countries regarding this form of 'vigilante justice'. The WTO DSU remedied this situation, as discussed in Section 8.5.1, by introducing reverse consensus decision-making for key steps in the dispute settlement process. It also introduced other reforms, including strict time frames and the possibility of appellate review. The DSU is considered to be one of the most important achievements of the Uruguay Round negotiations, and the WTO dispute settlement system has been called the 'jewel in the crown' of the WTO.

8.2 Object and purpose

According to Article 3.7 of the DSU, the prime object and purpose of the WTO dispute settlement system is to secure a positive solution to a dispute. The system therefore has a strong preference for solutions to disputes reached through consultations (i.e. negotiations) rather than adjudication. Amicable solutions are cheaper and better for the long-term trade relations between parties to the dispute than are adjudicated solutions. Only if consultations fail to achieve a mutually agreed solution may the dispute be brought before a WTO dispute settlement panel.

The dispute settlement system is essential in providing security and predictability to the multilateral trading system (Article 3.2 of the DSU). This objective has implications for the role of precedent in the WTO dispute settlement system (see Section 1.4).

> As held by the Appellate Body in *US – Stainless Steel (Mexico) (2008)*, ensuring security and predictability, as contemplated in Article 3.2 of the DSU, requires that, in the absence of cogent reasons, an adjudicatory body will resolve the same issues in the same way in a subsequent case.

The dispute settlement system further aims to ensure the resolution of disputes through multilateral procedures rather unilateral action. Article 23.1 of the DSU expressly requires Members to resort to the procedures set out in the DSU to redress violations of WTO law.

According to Article 3.2 of the DSU, the WTO dispute settlement system serves to preserve the rights and obligations of Members under the covered agreements (as defined in Section 8.3) and to clarify the existing provisions of those agreements. These clarifications must take place in accordance with the customary rules of interpretation of public international law, which are codified in Articles 31 and 32 of the Vienna Convention on the Law of Treaties (VCLT). According to these rules, panels and the Appellate

Body interpret the provisions of the covered agreements in good faith, in accordance with the ordinary meaning of the words of the provision, in their context and in the light of the object and purpose of the agreement involved. Where necessary or useful, recourse may be had to supplementary means of interpretation, such as the preparatory work of the agreement concerned or the circumstances of its conclusion.

> As held by the panel in *US – Section 301 Trade Act (2000)*, the elements referred to in Article 31 of the VCLT, namely text, context and object-and-purpose, as well as good faith, 'are to be viewed as one holistic rule of interpretation rather than a sequence of separate tests to be applied in a hierarchical order'.

There is much ambiguity in the provisions of WTO agreements in need of clarification. However, the nature and extent of the mandate of panels and the Appellate Body to 'clarify' the provisions of the WTO agreements is strictly limited. The DSU warns, in Articles 3.2 and 19.2, against judicial activism by specifying twice that WTO dispute settlement may not add to or diminish the rights and obligations of the WTO Members.

> As stated in a concurring opinion by an Appellate Body Member in *US – Continued Zeroing (2009)*, 'a treaty bears the imprint of many hands. And what is left behind is a text, sometimes negotiated to a point where an

agreement to regulate a matter could only be reached on the basis of constructive ambiguity, carrying both the hopes and fears of the parties. Interpretation is an endeavour to discern order, notwithstanding these infirmities, without adding to or diminishing the rights and obligations of the parties'.

8.3 Jurisdiction

The jurisdiction of the WTO dispute settlement system is very broad in scope. It covers all disputes arising under all the multilateral WTO agreements (except for the Trade Policy Review Mechanism) and the plurilateral Agreement on Government Procurement. These agreements are known as the 'covered agreements' (see Appendix 1 of the DSU). Disputes can thus concern a broad range of measures by WTO Members, including customs duties as well as the protection of copyrights, regulations affecting trade in services as well as phytosanitary measures, and anti-dumping duties as well as measures for the protection of the environment.

Furthermore, the jurisdiction of the WTO dispute settlement system is compulsory, exclusive and contentious in nature. It is *compulsory* because a WTO Member has no choice but to accept the system's jurisdiction when another WTO Member has brought a dispute. Unlike the situation before the International Court of Justice (ICJ), the responding party does not need to accept the jurisdiction of the WTO dispute settlement system to settle a dispute.

The jurisdiction of the WTO dispute settlement system is *exclusive* because, according to Article 23 of the DSU, a WTO Member that wants to bring a dispute under WTO law may only bring it to the WTO dispute settlement system. A WTO dispute can thus not be brought to the ICJ or any other adjudicatory body.

Finally, the *contentious* nature of the jurisdiction of the WTO dispute settlement system means that it is only called upon to clarify WTO law in the context of a specific dispute. It has no authority to issue advisory opinions.

8.4 Access

Access to the WTO dispute settlement system is limited to WTO Members. Neither the WTO Secretariat nor non-Members, international organizations, companies, civil society groups or individuals may bring disputes to the WTO dispute settlement system. In practice, however, almost all disputes are brought by a Member at the instigation of an affected industry or company. Companies or industry associations also often play an important behind the scenes role in planning the legal strategy and drafting the submissions in a dispute. They can thus be said to have 'indirect access' to the WTO dispute settlement system in this way.

Companies, individuals, civil society groups and others may also have 'indirect access' to the WTO dispute settlement system through the submission of *amicus curiae* briefs ('friends-of-the-court briefs') to panels or the Appellate Body. Although this issue is not addressed in the DSU, the Appellate Body has held that panels have discretion to accept and consider *amicus curiae* briefs based on their broad authority to seek information from any source (Article 13 of the DSU) and their authority to develop their own working procedures (Article 12 of the DSU), which together give panels extensive authority to control the process by which they inform themselves of the facts of a dispute and the legal norms applicable to it. This broad authority enables panels to conduct an 'objective assessment' of the matter before them as required by Article 11 of the DSU. The Appellate Body has held that its own discretion to accept and consider *amicus curiae* briefs rests on its broad authority to adopt procedural rules that do not conflict with the DSU or covered agreements, as provided in Article 17.9 of the DSU and Rule 16.1 of the Working Procedures for Appellate Review. However, there has been fierce opposition by WTO Members, particularly developing-country Members, to the acceptance of *amicus curiae* briefs in WTO dispute settlement. To date, panels have sparingly, and the Appellate Body has never, made use of their discretion to do so.

A WTO Member can have recourse to the WTO dispute settlement system if it considers that a benefit accruing to it under one of the covered agreements has been nullified or impaired (Article XXIII:1 of the GATT 1994). A complainant will almost always argue that the respondent violated a provision of WTO law (violation complaint), in which case nullification or impairment of benefits is presumed (Article 3.8 of the DSU). However, the nullification or impairment of benefits could also be the consequence of a measure or situation that is not in conflict with WTO law (a non-violation complaint or a situation complaint, as provided for in Articles 26.1 and 26.2 of the DSU). In the case of non-violation or situation complaints, the complainant will have to prove that there is nullification or impairment of a benefit. There have been no successful non-violation complaints under the DSU to date, and no situation complaint has ever been adjudicated. Therefore these two additional causes of action are of little practical significance.

WTO Members have broad discretion in deciding whether to bring a case against another Member. Article 3.7 of the DSU requires a Member to 'exercise its judgement' as to whether action under the procedures of the DSU 'would be fruitful' before bringing a case. However, Members are largely self-regulating in applying this requirement because panels are not authorized to question a Member's exercise of its judgment as to whether recourse to the panel would be 'fruitful'.

As recognized by the Appellate Body in *EC – Bananas III (1997)*, 'with the increased interdependence of the global economy, Members have a greater stake in enforcing WTO rules than in the past since any deviation from the negotiated balance of rights and obligations is more likely than ever to affect them, directly or indirectly'. In that case, despite the fact that the United States was not an exporter of bananas, it was held to be entitled to bring a complaint of inconsistency with GATT obligations against the EU's preferential import regime for bananas from ACP countries because it was a potential exporter of bananas.

Despite the self-regulating nature of the requirement of Article 3.7 of the DSU, it is apparent from the 90 per cent success rate of WTO complaints that Members do duly exercise their judgment as to whether bringing a WTO dispute will be fruitful.

Aside from the parties to a dispute, other Members may have access to WTO dispute settlement proceedings. Any Member that has a 'substantial interest' in a dispute and has notified this interest to the DSB in a timely manner may become a 'third party' in the panel proceedings (Article 10 of the DSU), and any third party in panel proceedings may become a 'third participant' in Appellate Body proceedings (Article 17.4 of the DSU). Third parties and third participants have the *right* to be heard by the panel and the Appellate Body, respectively. Third parties' rights are rather limited: they may present their views in a special session of the first substantive meeting of the panel with the parties, they receive the first written submissions of the parties and they may make one written submission. Exceptionally, for instance, when they have a major interest in the outcome of the dispute, third parties may be granted 'enhanced third party rights' by the panel. In contrast, the rights of third participants in appellate proceedings are more extensive: they receive all written submissions, may file a written submission and may participate in the oral hearing of the Appellate Body with the participants.

WTO Members have discretion to determine the composition of their own delegations in WTO dispute settlement proceedings. They thus may, and frequently do, make use of private legal counsel to represent them in these proceedings.

8.5 Dispute settlement organs

Among the institutions involved in WTO dispute settlement, one can distinguish between a political institution, the Dispute Settlement Body (DSB), and two independent, judicial-type institutions: the ad hoc dispute settlement panels and the permanent Appellate Body. Each of these is discussed next.

8.5.1 The Dispute Settlement Body

The DSB is composed of all WTO Members and administers the dispute settlement system (see Section 7.4). According to Article 2.1 of the DSU, the DSB has the authority:

- to establish panels;
- to adopt panel and Appellate Body reports (through which the 'recommendations and rulings' in these reports become legally binding);
- to supervise the implementation of the 'recommendations and rulings' made in panel and Appellate Body reports; and
- to authorize the suspension of concessions and other obligations under the covered agreements (i.e. the taking of retaliation measures) if a WTO Member does not implement the adopted 'recommendations and rulings' within a specified reasonable period of time.

This may lead one to conclude that, even though the settlement of disputes is conducted by panels and the Appellate Body, the DSB (i.e. the political organ) controls the whole process, thus undermining its judicial nature. It must be noted, however, that the decisions on the establishment of panels, on the adoption of panel and Appellate Body reports and on the authorization of retaliation measures are taken by the DSB by *reverse consensus*. This means that the DSB is considered to have taken decisions on these matters unless there is consensus among Members *not* to take the relevant decision. It is clear that such a consensus is highly improbable because the Member who puts the request for the decision on the agenda of the DSB is very unlikely to join a consensus not to adopt the decision. In other words, the decisions made by the DSB on these matters are for all practical purposes made automatically.

8.5.2 *Panels*

Panels are ad hoc bodies established for the purpose of adjudicating a particular dispute and are dissolved once they have accomplished this task. As specified in Article 6 of the DSU, panels are established by the DSB by reverse consensus, at the request of the complainant, at the latest at the second meeting of the DSB in which the panel request is on the agenda.

After the establishment of the panel, the parties decide on its composition on the basis of proposals made by the WTO Secretariat. However, if they fail to reach agreement on the composition of the panel within twenty days after its establishment, either party may ask the Director-General of the WTO to appoint the panelists. The Director-General does so within ten days of the request (Article 8.7 of the DSU). In recent years, most panels have been composed by the Director-General.

In general, panels are composed of three well-qualified governmental and/or non-governmental individuals (such as

271

diplomats or trade officials; less commonly, academics or prac-
ticing lawyers) (Article 8.1 of the DSU). Panelists may not be
nationals of the parties or third parties to the dispute unless the
parties agree otherwise (Article 8.3 of the DSU).

Panelists serve in their individual capacities, not as
government representatives (Article 8.9 of the DSU). They are
subject to the Rules of Conduct for WTO dispute settlement
when hearing a WTO dispute. The Rules of Conduct require
panelists to be independent and impartial, to avoid direct or
indirect conflicts of interest and to respect the confidentiality
of the proceedings. To ensure compliance with these obligations, panelists are required to disclose any interest, relationship or matter that affects or creates justifiable doubts as to
their independence or impartiality. Parties can request the
DSB Chair to disqualify a panelist on the grounds of material
violation of the Rules of Conduct. To date, no panelist has
ever been disqualified, but very rarely a panelist has volunta-
rily withdrawn from a panel after a party raised concerns
regarding a possible conflict of interests.

8.5.3 The Appellate Body

The Appellate Body is a standing (i.e. permanent) international tribunal of seven independent persons of recognized
authority in law, international trade and the subject matter of
the covered agreements generally (Articles 17.1 and 17.3 of the
DSU). The Members of the Appellate Body are appointed by
the DSB for a term of four years, renewable only once (Article
17.2 of the DSU). The composition of the Appellate Body must
be broadly representative of the WTO membership.

The Appellate Body is currently composed of Ujal Singh Bhatia (India), Peter Van den Bossche (Belgium), Seung Wha Chang (Korea), Thomas R. Graham (United States), Ricardo Ramírez-Hernándes (Mexico), Shree Baboo Chekitan Servansing (Mauritius) and Yuejiao Zhang (China).

Appellate Body Members may not be affiliated with any government (Article 17.3 of the DSU). They may also not accept any employment or pursue any professional activities that are inconsistent with their duties as Appellate Body Members (Rule 2(2) of the Working Procedures for Appellate Review).

The Appellate Body hears and decides appeals in divisions of three of its Members. The Appellate Body Members constituting a Division to hear an appeal are selected on the basis of rotation, taking into account the principles of random selection and unpredictability and the opportunity for all Members to serve regardless of their nationality (Rule 6(2) of the Working Procedures for Appellate Review).

Appellate Body Members are bound by the Rules of Conduct. They are thus, like panelists, required to be independent and impartial, to avoid direct or indirect conflicts of interest and to respect the confidentiality of the proceedings. They must disclose the existence of development of any interest, relationship or matter that is likely to affect or give rise to justifiable doubts as to their independence and impartiality. They may not participate in the consideration of an appeal that would create a direct or indirect conflict of interests. Parties can request the Appellate Body to disqualify one of its Members on grounds of material violation of the Rules of Conduct. No such request has ever been made to date.

Whereas an appeal is decided by the Division assigned to that appeal, in the interests of consistency and coherence in WTO case law, in each appeal an exchange of views on the issues raised by the appeal is held with the Appellate Body Members who are not on the Division.

8.6 Procedural arrangements

The WTO dispute settlement process comprises four major steps:

- compulsory consultations between the parties to a dispute to try to reach a mutually agreed solution;
- panel proceedings;
- appellate review proceedings; and
- implementation and enforcement of the recommendations and rulings adopted by the DSB.

These steps are illustrated by the flowchart in Figure 8.1, prepared by the WTO Secretariat, and are discussed further herein.

8.6.1 Consultations

Reflecting the preference of the WTO dispute settlement system for mutually agreed solutions to disputes, rather than

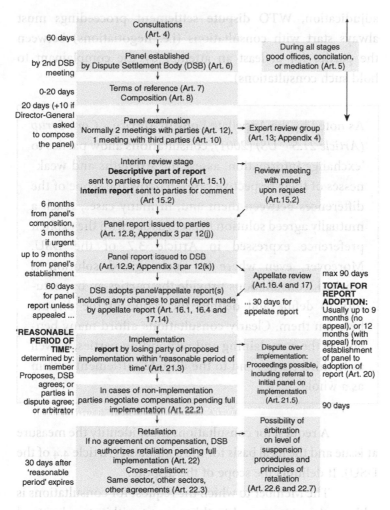

Figure 8.1: Flowchart of WTO dispute settlement process (source: WTO website)

adjudication, WTO dispute settlement proceedings must always start with consultations (i.e. negotiations) between the parties (or at least an attempt by the complainant to hold such consultations).

> As noted by the Appellate Body in *Mexico – Corn Syrup (Article 21.5 – US) (2001)*, consultations allow parties to 'exchange information, assess the strengths and weaknesses of their respective cases, narrow the scope of the differences between them and, in many cases, reach a mutually agreed solution in accordance with the explicit preference expressed in Article 3.7 of the DSU. Moreover, even where no such agreed solution is reached, consultations provide the parties an opportunity to define and delimit the scope of the dispute between them. Clearly consultations afford many benefits to the complaining and responding parties, as well as to third parties and to the dispute settlement system as a whole'.

A request for consultations must identify the measure at issue and the legal basis for the complaint (Article 4.4 of the DSU). It delimits the scope of the dispute.

The Member to which the request for consultations is addressed must respond to this request within ten days and enter into consultations within thirty days of the receipt of the request (Article 4.3 of the DSU). If it does not do so, the requesting Member may proceed directly to request the establishment of a panel to hear the dispute. Otherwise, consultations are held for a minimum of sixty days, unless the parties agree within the sixty-day period that the consultations have failed to resolve the dispute (Article 4.7 of the DSU).

Consultations are confidential and without prejudice to the rights of any Member in further proceedings (Article 4.6 of the DSU). Although Members are required to engage in consultations in good faith, there is no public record of the consultations and panels are not authorized to assess the adequacy of consultations. Panels may only determine whether consultations were held. If the respondent raises the lack of consultations in a timely manner, the panel would have to conclude that it has no jurisdiction to hear the dispute.

It is possible for other Members that have a 'substantial trade interest' in the dispute to join the consultations provided that the consultations were initiated under Article XXII (rather than Article XXIII) of the GATT 1994 and that the respondent agrees.

If consultations are successful, the mutually agreed solution achieved must be notified to the DSB and be consistent with WTO law (Articles 3.5 and 3.6 of the DSU). One in five disputes are resolved through consultations. If consultations are unsuccessful in resolving the dispute within sixty days of receipt of the request for consultations, the complainant may request the establishment of a panel to hear the dispute. However, often, the complainant will allow more time for consultations before proceeding to requesting a panel to be established.

8.6.2 *Panel proceedings*

If consultations are unsuccessful in resolving a dispute, a complainant may proceed to request the establishment of a panel. As noted earlier, a panel will be established by reverse consensus at the latest at the second DSB meeting at which this request is on the agenda.

Almost all panels have standard terms of reference, which refer back to the complainant's request for the establishment of a panel (Article 7.1 of the DSU). The request for the establishment of a panel must therefore clearly identify the measure at issue and set out the claims of violation of WTO law (Article 6.2 of the DSU). A measure or a claim falls within the panel's terms of reference (i.e. within the jurisdiction of the panel) only if that measure or that claim is sufficiently identified in the panel request. A panel is bound by its terms of reference and may not examine measures or claims falling outside it. If this were not so, a respondent would not be able to prepare a proper defense, and therefore its due process rights would be violated.

Agricola requested the establishment of a panel to hear a dispute regarding Industria's minimum price requirements for chocolate bars, which Agricola claimed to be in violation of Article XI:1 of the GATT 1994. However, in its written submission to the panel, Agricola now argues that the minimum price requirements violate not only Article XI:1 but also Article III:4 of the GATT 1994 because they result de facto in less favourable treatment of imports of chocolate bars than of domestic chocolate. Agricola further argues that not only do Industria's minimum price requirements for chocolate bars violate Article XI:1 of the GATT 1994, but also its requirement that chocolate bars be imported through only one port of entry violates this article. Because the panel is bound by its terms of reference as set out in Agricola's request for the establishment of the panel, the claim of a violation of Article III:4 of the GATT 1994 and the challenge to the port of entry requirement for imports of chocolate bars are outside its jurisdiction and thus cannot be considered by the panel.

The basic Working Procedures for panels are set out in Appendix 3 to the DSU, and panels are free to (and usually do) adopt, in consultation with the parties, more detailed ad hoc working procedures for purposes of the dispute before them (Article 12 of the DSU).

The function of a panel is 'to make an objective assessment of the matter before it, including an objective assessment of the facts of the case and the applicability of, and conformity with, the relevant covered agreements' (Article 11 of the DSU). A panel must consider all the evidence before it in an even-handed manner and base its findings on sufficient factual evidence. However, this does not mean that a panel has to accord to evidence the weight that a party believes it should be accorded. A panel has discretion as the trier of facts to determine that certain evidence should be accorded more weight than other evidence.

Frequently, complainants allege several violations of various WTO agreements with regard to the same measure. Panels are not obliged to address each claim made by the complainant but are entitled to exercise judicial economy.

According to the Appellate Body in *US – Wool Shirts and Blouses (1997)*, panels 'need only address those claims which must be addressed in order to resolve the matter in issue in the dispute'.

However, panels should guard against 'false judicial economy'. The claims that are not addressed by the panel may give rise to a new dispute. Panels must therefore address all claims on which a finding is necessary to ensure the effective resolution of the dispute.

Panel proceedings often involve complex factual, technical or scientific issues. In such cases, panels regularly consult experts to obtain their advice on the issues under consideration. A panel has broad discretion to seek information from any individual or body that it deems appropriate (Article 13 of the DSU) in order to help the panel understand and evaluate the evidence and arguments brought by the parties. The panel may not use information obtained from its experts to make the case for one of the parties. Experts consulted by the panel are bound by the Rules of Conduct and must therefore be independent and impartial.

A panel must submit its findings to the DSB in the form of a written report containing its findings of fact, its findings on the applicability of the relevant legal provisions and the basic rationale for its findings and recommendations (Article 12.7 of the DSU). Before finalizing its report, a panel will share the draft of the report with the parties for their comments (Article 15 of the DSU). During this so-called *interim review*, parties will often and primarily suggest the correction of factual errors that they consider the panel made. The final version of the panel report is first issued to the parties to the dispute and then, after translation into the remaining two of the three official languages of the WTO (English, French and Spanish), is circulated to all Members and published on the WTO website. The recommendations and rulings of a panel contained in the panel report only become binding once they have been adopted by the DSB. This occurs within sixty days of the circulation of the panel report unless a party notifies its decision to appeal. As discussed in Section 8.5.1, the decision to adopt a panel report is taken by the DSB by reverse consensus and is thus quasi-automatic.

8.6.3 *Appellate review*

At any time after the circulation and before the adoption of a panel report, a party to a dispute can initiate appellate review proceedings against the panel report before the Appellate Body by means of a notice of appeal (Article 17 of the DSU). The notice of appeal sets out the findings or legal interpretations of the panel that are being appealed. It is possible, and often happens, that once a party to the dispute appeals certain aspects of the panel report, the other party files a 'notice of other appeal'; that is, it 'cross-appeals' other aspects of the panel report. The notice of appeal and the notice of other appeal delimit the Appellate Body's terms of reference for the relevant appeal. Third parties may not appeal a panel report but may participate as 'third participants' in Appellate Body proceedings (see Section 8.4).

Unlike panels, the Appellate Body has detailed standard Working Procedures for Appellate Review, which it has drawn up under the authority granted to it by Article 17.9 of the DSU. When a procedural issue arises that is not addressed in the DSU or these Working Procedures, the Division hearing an appeal may, 'in the interests of fairness and orderly procedure in the conduct of an appeal', adopt an appropriate procedural rule for the purposes of that appeal (Rule 16(1) of the Working Procedures).

An appeal is limited to issues of law covered in the panel report and legal interpretations developed by the panel (Article 17.6 of the DSU). Issues of fact cannot be appealed. However, a finding involving the application of a legal rule to the facts is a legal characterization of these facts and thus a finding on an issue of law subject to appellate review. Moreover, although issues of fact cannot be appealed, factual findings may be appealed on the ground that the panel failed to make an objective assessment of the facts as required under Article 11 of the DSU (see Section 8.6.2). However, in view of the different roles of panels and the Appellate Body, the Appellate Body will not lightly interfere with the fact-finding authority of a panel and will not overturn such a finding purely on the basis that it might have reached a different factual conclusion than the one the panel reached.

> For example, a finding of the panel that Industria has minimum price requirements in place for chocolate bars is a factual finding and cannot be appealed. A finding that such minimum price requirements have a limiting effect on importation and are thus 'restrictions' on importation for purposes of Article XI of the GATT 1994 entails the application of a legal rule to the facts and is subject to appeal. Furthermore, the panel's failure to consider the evidence brought by Industria contesting the existence of minimum price requirements for chocolate bars could be challenged on appeal as a failure to conduct an 'objective assessment', as required by Article 11 of the DSU.

The Appellate Body may uphold, modify or reverse the legal findings and conclusions of a panel (Article 17.13 of the DSU). However, in some cases, the Appellate Body has gone further than this mandate and has 'completed the legal analysis' of the panel. It has done so where this was necessary to avoid leaving the dispute unresolved, for example, in cases where it has overturned the findings of the panel with regard to specific claims and the panel had exercised judicial economy with regard to other claims, or in cases where the panel wrongly found that a provision was not applicable to the measure at issue. In such cases, due to the absence of remand authority in WTO dispute settlement, the dispute would have remained unresolved had the Appellate Body not proceeded to address the remaining claims or to apply the relevant provision to the measure at issue.

> The panel in a dispute brought by Industria regarding a technical requirement imposed by Agricola on smartphones finds that the requirement constitutes a violation of Article 2.1 of the TBT Agreement. It then decides to exercise judicial economy with regard to Industria's additional claim that the requirement also violates Article 2.2 of the TBT Agreement. On appeal, the Appellate Body overturns the panel's finding of a violation of Article 2.1 of the TBT Agreement. If the Appellate Body would not proceed to complete the legal analysis by addressing Industria's claim under Article 2.2, the dispute would remain unresolved.

The Appellate Body will only complete the legal analysis in limited cases, namely when it is necessary to resolve the dispute, there are sufficient factual findings in the panel report or undisputed facts on which to base its legal analysis and the claims are not 'novel'. A claim is 'novel' when it concerns an issue not yet dealt with in WTO dispute settlement at all or when it concerns an issue not fully explored before the panel or in the course of the Appellate Body proceedings. In such situations, the Appellate Body would not complete the legal analysis out of consideration for parties' due process rights.

> In *EC – Seal Products (2014)*, the panel had found that the EU Seal Regime fell within the scope of application of the TBT Agreement because it was covered by the definition of a 'technical regulation', namely, a

'[d]ocument which lays down product characteristics or their related processes and production methods, ... with which compliance is mandatory'. In particular, the panel found that the Seal Regime laid down 'product characteristics'. It exercised judicial economy regarding the question of whether the Seal Regime laid down 'related processes and production methods'. On appeal, the Appellate Body overturned the panel's decision that the Seal Regime laid down product characteristics. However, citing the 'important systemic issues' entailed, it declined to complete the legal analysis by addressing whether the Seal Regime nevertheless fell within the scope of application of the TBT Agreement as a document laying down 'related processes and production methods'. According to the Appellate Body, the claim raised issues of a novel character that had not been explored by the panel at all, and on which the parties had not focused their argumentation, giving rise to concerns about the parties' due process rights.

Once an Appellate Body report is finalized, it is translated so that it is available in the three official languages of the WTO and then circulated to all WTO Members and published on the WTO website. Within thirty days following the circulation of the Appellate Body report, the Appellate Body report and the panel report, as upheld, modified or reversed by the Appellate Body, are adopted by the DSB by reverse consensus (Article 17.14 of the DSU). When these reports have been adopted by the DSB, they become legally binding.

8.6.4 Implementation and enforcement

When a panel and/or the Appellate Body concludes that the responding Member acted inconsistently with its WTO obligations and the DSB adopts the panel and/or Appellate Body reports, the responding Member must bring its measure into conformity with WTO law and it must do so promptly (Article 21.1 of the DSU). If that is impracticable, the Member concerned must do so within a 'reasonable period of time' (Article 21.3 of the DSU). Most often, parties reach agreement on the length of the 'reasonable period of time' for implementation, but if agreement proves impossible within forty-five days, the matter may be referred to arbitration (Article 21.3(c) of the DSU). In such cases, the arbitrator decides on the reasonable period of time for implementation, taking into account the legal system of the responding Member and the means and complexity of the implementation. In practice, the reasonable period granted for implementation typically varies between six and fifteen months. The DSB keeps under surveillance the implementation of the recommendations and rulings it has adopted (Articles 21.6 and 22.8 of the DSU).

It regularly happens that the complainant and respondent disagree as to the existence or WTO-consistency of measures taken to comply with the recommendations and rulings of the DSB. According to Article 21.5 of the DSU, any such disagreement – commonly referred to as a 'compliance dispute' – must be resolved according to basically the same dispute settlement procedures as those set out earlier, but subject to shorter time frames. The reports of the panel and

Appellate Body in compliance disputes become binding upon adoption by the DSB, by reverse consensus.

Although 'prompt compliance' through the modification or withdrawal of the WTO-inconsistent measure is the only final remedy for breach of WTO law, the DSU provides for two temporary remedies in case of non-compliance: namely, compensation and retaliation. If the respondent has failed to implement the recommendations and rulings of the DSB correctly within the 'reasonable period of time', the respondent must, if so requested by the complainant, enter into negotiations to agree on mutually acceptable compensation (Article 22.2 of the DSU). Compensation does not address past damage but is forward-looking, concerning the nullification or impairment of benefits from expiry of the reasonable period of time for implementation until implementation occurs. If, as is usually the case, agreement on compensation cannot be reached within twenty days of the expiry of the reasonable period of time, the complainant may request authorization from the DSB to suspend an equivalent level of concessions or other obligations with regard to the respondent Member; in other words, authorization to take retaliation measures (Article 22.2 of the DSU). As mentioned in Section 8.5.1, the DSB gives its authorization by reverse consensus, thus quasi-automatically.

The level of retaliation may not exceed the level of the benefit being nullified or impaired by the WTO-inconsistent measure (Article 22.4 of the DSU). Disputes regarding the level of retaliation are brought to arbitration, usually conducted by the members of the original panel (Article 22.6 of the DSU).

> The levels of retaliation awarded under Article 22.6 arbitration to date range between US$21 million per year to Antigua and Barbuda in *US – Gambling (Article 22.6 – US) (2007)* and US$4.043 million per year to the European Communities in *US – FSC (Article 22.6 – US) (2002)*.

Retaliation measures usually take the form of a drastic increase in custom duties on strategically selected products exported by the responding Member, as was the case in *EC – Bananas III (1997)* and *EC – Hormones (1998)*. Retaliation may alternatively take the form of suspension of 'obligations' rather than of tariff concessions, for example, by withdrawing protection of intellectual property rights relating to products produced in the responding Member. Authorization to retaliate in this manner was granted in *US – Gambling (2005), US – Upland Cotton (2005)* and *EC – Bananas III (1997)*. In those cases in which retaliation measures were actually applied, the products affected by the retaliation measures were typically unrelated to the products at issue in the dispute. Not surprisingly, the producers of the affected products exerted heavy pressure on the respondent Member's government to withdraw or amend the WTO-inconsistent measure as quickly as possible.

Retaliation measures are by nature trade-destructive and have a negative effect not only on the responding Member's economy, but also that of the Member applying these measures. Consequently, retaliation is often not a feasible option for developing-country complainants to enforce compliance with the recommendations and rulings in a dispute. However, it should be noted that, in the large majority of disputes, responding Members comply with the outcome of dispute settlement without the need for retaliation.

> In 85 per cent of all disputes in which a WTO-inconsistent measure must be amended or withdrawn, the respondent complies with the recommendations and rulings of the DSB. In only 15 per cent of these disputes is the implementation of the recommendations and rulings a problem.

8.7 Key features of the proceedings

8.7.1 Strict timeframes

WTO dispute settlement proceedings are characterized by strict time limits, in contrast to other international courts such as the ICJ or the International Tribunal on the Law of the Sea (ITLOS). Although these time limits have been criticized as excessively short and demanding, the need for prompt settlement of WTO disputes is clear from the fact that there is no possibility in the WTO dispute settlement system for compensation for the harm suffered as a result of WTO-inconsistent measures during the period that the dispute is ongoing.

According to Article 12.9 of the DSU, panel proceedings, from the date of establishment of the panel to the circulation of the panel report, should not exceed nine months. Even shorter time frames apply in cases of urgency:

for example, in disputes involving perishable goods (Article 12.8 of the DSU), in disputes involving subsidies (Articles 4 and 7 of the SCM Agreement) and in compliance disputes (Article 21.5 of the DSU). In practice, however, most panel proceedings exceed the prescribed periods. Delays are, *inter alia*, due to the complexity of the cases, the need to consult experts, scheduling problems and the time needed to translate lengthy reports.

The DSU provides that Appellate Body proceedings shall in no case take longer than ninety days (Article 17.5 of the DSU). Whereas, for many years, the Appellate Body only exceptionally deviated from this strict time frame, the recent increase in the number and – even more so – in the scope and complexity of appeals has, however, made it impossible for the Appellate Body to circulate its report in all appeals within the ninety-day timeframe.

With regard to reports adopted in 2013 and 2014, the average time taken by panels between their establishment and the circulation of their report was 445 days (14 months and 19 days). The average time taken by the Appellate Body in this period between the notice of appeal and the circulation of the Appellate Body report was 108 days.

8.7.2 *Confidentiality*

Unlike most national and international judicial proceedings, WTO dispute settlement proceedings are confidential. This confidentiality requirement relates to submissions to panels and the Appellate Body (Article 18.2 of the DSU), the meetings of panels with the parties (paragraph 2 of Appendix 3 of the DSU) and the hearings of the Appellate Body (Article 17.10 of the DSU) and panel reports before they are circulated to all Members. The confidentiality of the WTO dispute settlement process is considered vital by some Members, whereas the lack of transparency resulting from such confidentiality has been harshly criticized by other Members and civil society.

Despite the requirement of confidentiality of submissions, parties to a dispute are free to forego confidentiality in respect of their statements of position and make their own written submissions public (Article 18.2, second sentence of the DSU). A party may also request a non-confidential summary of the opposing party's submission to disclose to the public (Article 18.2, last sentence of the DSU). However, due to the lack of a deadline by which non-confidential summaries must be provided, this provision is of little practical use.

Because sensitive business confidential information (BCI) may be relevant evidence in a WTO dispute, in certain cases, panels and the Appellate Body have adopted special procedures to protect the confidentiality of this information.

In *EC and Certain Member States – Large Civil Aircraft (2011)*, the dispute involving billions of euros of subsidies to Airbus, the Appellate Body provided for detailed additional procedures for the protection of BCI and highly sensitive business information (HSBI). To protect HSBI, the additional procedures required, *inter alia*, that:

'[a]ll HSBI shall be stored in a combination safe in a designated secure location on the premises of the Appellate Body Secretariat. Any computer in that room shall be a stand-alone computer, that is, not connected to a network. Appellate Body Members and assigned Appellate Body Secretariat staff may view HSBI only in the designated secure location referred to above'.

Despite the provisions in the DSU requiring the confidentiality of panel meetings and Appellate Body hearings, some Members hold the view that these should be opened to the public. At the request of parties to the dispute, the panels, in certain cases, have decided to open up panel meetings to the public, relying on their authority under Article 12.1 of the DSU to deviate from the working procedures for panels set out in Appendix 3 of the DSU. Similarly, at the request of the parties to some disputes, the Appellate Body has opened up its hearings to the public. It has done so on the basis of the right of parties to forego confidentiality in respect of their statements of position (Article 18.2 of the DSU) and its own authority to control the conduct of its oral hearings (Rule 27 of the Working Procedures of the Appellate Body). When the Appellate Body allows public observation of its hearings, it does so by means of closed-circuit television broadcast to a separate viewing room at WTO Headquarters in Geneva. To safeguard the rights of confidentiality of those third participants that did not agree to public observation, the transmission is turned off during statements made by those third participants.

8.7.3 Burden of proof

There are no specific rules on the burden of proof in the DSU. However, the Appellate Body has held that the rules on burden of proof that apply in various international tribunals, including the ICJ, and most national jurisdictions, apply also in WTO dispute settlement. According to these rules, the burden of proof is on the party, whether complainant or respondent, that asserts the affirmative of a claim or defense. When a prima facie case has been made (i.e. sufficient evidence has been adduced to raise a presumption that what is claimed is true), the burden shifts to the opposing party to rebut this evidence. When a respondent raises an exception as an affirmative defense, it bears the burden of proof with regard to that exception. The task of a panel is to balance all the evidence on record and establish whether the party bearing the ultimate burden of proof (i.e. the complainant) has convinced it of the validity of its claims.

Note that the burden of establishing what the applicable rule of WTO law is and how that rule must be interpreted is not on the parties but, consistent with the principle of *jura novit curia*, on the panel and the Appellate Body.

8.8 Developing countries and dispute settlement

Although developing countries actively make use of the WTO dispute settlement system, their lack of knowledge of and experience in WTO law may form an important barrier to their use of this system. This is particularly so for the smaller developing countries.

In recognition of the difficulties developing-country Members may encounter when they are involved in WTO dispute settlement, the DSU contains special rules for these Members. For example, in the case of developing-country respondents, the time period for consultations may be extended and they may, under certain circumstances, be granted more time to file their written submissions to a panel (Article 12.10 of the DSU). Also, the WTO Secretariat has appointed two advisors who can assist, to some extent, developing-country Members in their disputes (Article 27 of the DSU). Finally, note that in disputes with developed-country Members, developing-country Members have the right to have a developing-country national as a member of the panel (Article 8.10 of the DSU). Most of the DSU rules providing for special and differential treatment for developing-country Members are, however, of limited practical significance.

Effective legal assistance to developing-country Members in dispute settlement proceedings is provided by the Advisory Centre on WTO Law (ACWL). The ACWL is a Geneva-based, independent, international organization established and financed by a number of developed and developing countries. The ACWL gives its developing-country members and all LDCs legal advice on WTO law at discounted rates, and it regularly represents developing-country Members in procedures before a panel or the Appellate Body.

Further reading

Alschner, W. (2014) 'Amicable settlements of WTO disputes: bilateral solutions in a multilateral system', *World Trade Review* 13 65–102.

Bartels, L., 'Jurisdiction and applicable law in the WTO' (October 1, 2014) *University of Cambridge Faculty of Law Research Paper No. 59/2014* available at http://ssrn.com/abstract=2500684

Bohanes, J., and Garza, F. (2012) 'Going beyond stereotypes: participation of developing countries in WTO dispute settlement', *Trade, Law and Development* 4(1) 45–124.

Davey, J. W. (2014) 'The WTO and rules-based dispute settlement: historical evolution, operational success and future challenges', *Journal of International Economic Law* 17 679–700.

Tijmes, J. (2014) 'Jurisprudential developments on the purpose of WTO suspension of obligations' *World Trade Review*, 13 1–38.

Van Damme, I. (2010) 'Treaty interpretation by the WTO Appellate Body', *The European Journal of International Law* 21(3) 605–648.

Voon, T., and Yanovich, A. (2006) 'Facts aside: the limitation of WTO appeals to issues of law' *Journal of World Trade*, 40(2) 239–258.

Zimmermann, D. C. (2012) 'The neglected link between the legal nature of WTO rules, the political filtering of WTO disputes, and the absence of retrospective WTO remedies', *Trade Law and Development* 4(1) 251–267.

Bridges Weekly Trade News Digest:

http://www.ictsd.org/bridges-news/bridges/overview

Bridges is a publication of the International Centre for Trade and Sustainable Development (ICTSD). It is a leading source of accurate, objective and timely information on international trade and sustainable development issues. Bridges is disseminated every Thursday to its subscribers via email, free of charge.

Harmonized System Nomenclature of the World Customs Organization:

http://www.wcoomd.org/en/topics/nomenclature/instrument-and-tools/hs_nomenclature_2012/hs_nomenclature_table_2012.aspx

The World Customs Organization provides a link to the 2012 edition of the Harmonized Commodity Description and Coding System Nomenclature (Harmonised System or HS Nomenclature).

Integrated Trade Intelligence Portal (I-TIP) Goods:

https://i-tip.wto.org/goods/default.aspx?language=en

The I-TIP Goods is an initiative of the WTO and provides comprehensive information on non-tariff measures (NTMs) applied by WTO Members in merchandise trade. The information includes Members' notifications of NTMs as well as information on "specific trade concerns" raised by Members at WTO committee meetings. Its aim is to serve the needs of those seeking detailed information on trade policy measures as well as those looking for summary information. It includes links to the WTO's extensive tariff and trade databases, and to the DocsOnLine system.

Integrated Trade Intelligence Portal (I-TIP) Services: http://i-tip.wto.org/services/(S(20nbdfzztzlfc4lgoozrovdc))/default.aspx

The I-TIPS Services is a joint initiative of the WTO and the World Bank. It is a set of linked databases that provides information on Members' commitments under the WTO's General Agreement on Trade in Services (GATS), services commitments in regional trade agreements (RTAs), applied measures in services and services statistics.

International Economic Law and Policy Blog: http://worldtradelaw.typepad.com/ielpblog

This blog offers commentary by leading experts on current developments and scholarship in the field of international economic law and policy.

Regional Trade Agreements Information System (RTA-IS): http://rtais.wto.org/UI/PublicMaintainRTAHome.aspx

This WTO database contains information on only those agreements that have either been notified or for which an early announcement has been made to the WTO. It allows you to retrieve information on RTAs by country/ territory or by criteria. You may also consult the list of all RTAs in force, the list of early announcements and the pre- defined reports and summary tables containing WTO fig- ures on RTAs.

Schedules of Concessions of WTO Members:
http://www.wto.org/english/tratop_e/schedules_e/goods_sche dules_table_e.htm

The GATT 1994 Schedules of Concessions (Goods Schedules) of all WTO Members can be accessed through this page of the WTO website.

Schedules of Specific Commitments of WTO Members:
http://www.wto.org/english/tratop_e/serv_e/serv_commit ments_e.htm

The GATS Schedules of Specific Commitments (Services Schedules) of all WTO Members as well as the lists of MFN treatment exemptions under Article II:2 of the GATS can be accessed through this page of the WTO website.

TARIC database of the European Union:
http://ec.europa.eu/taxation_customs/customs/customs_du ties/tariff_aspects/customs_tariff/index_en.htm

TARIC, the integrated Tariff of the European Union, is a multilingual database in which are integrated all mea- sures relating to EU customs tariff, commercial and agri- cultural legislation. By integrating and coding these measures, the TARIC secures their uniform application by all Member States and gives all economic operators a clear view of all measures to be undertaken when importing into the EU or exporting goods from the EU. It also makes it possible to collect EU-wide statistics for the measures concerned.

Tariff Analysis Online Facility (TAO):
https://tariffanalysis.wto.org/welcome.aspx?ReturnUrl=%2f%3fui%3d1&ui=1

This facility allows you to access the WTO's Integrated Data Base (IDB) and Consolidated Tariff Schedules (CTS) database online, select markets and products, compile reports and download data. It contains applied customs duties at the tariff line level, import statistics by country of origin and WTO Members' commitments on goods (bound tariffs and specific commitments in agriculture).

Tariff Download Facility:
http://tariffdata.wto.org/Default.aspx?culture=en-US

This WTO database contains comprehensive information on most-favoured-nation (MFN) applied and bound tariffs at the standard codes of the Harmonized System (HS) for all WTO Members. When available, it also provides data at the HS subheading level on non-MFN applied tariff regimes that a country grants to its export partners. This information is sourced from submissions made to the WTO's Integrated Data Base (IDB) for applied tariffs and imports and from the Consolidated Tariff Schedules (CTS) database for the bound duties of all WTO Members.

Worldtradelaw.net:

www.worldtradelaw.net

Worldtradelaw.net offers both a free resource library of current trade news and resources, as well as a subscription service (the Dispute Settlement Commentary Service), which provides summary and analysis of all WTO reports and arbitrations; a current keyword index; a database of dispute settlement tables and statistics and a user-friendly search tool for WTO cases, legal texts and other documents.

WTO Analytical Index: Guide to WTO Law and Practice:

http://www.wto.org/english/res_e/booksp_e/analytic_index_e/analytic_index_e.htm

The WTO Analytical Index is a comprehensive guide to the interpretation and application of the WTO agreements by the Appellate Body, dispute settlement panels and other WTO bodies. It contains extracts of key pronouncements and findings from tens of thousands of pages of WTO jurisprudence, including panel reports, Appellate Body reports, arbitral decisions and awards, and decisions of WTO committees, councils and other WTO bodies.

WTO Analytical Index Supplement Covering New Developments in WTO Law and Practice:

http://www.wto.org/english/res_e/booksp_e/analytic_index_e/ai_new_dev_e.pdf

This supplement covers developments in WTO law and practice after 30 September 2011. It is updated in electronic form on an ongoing basis to reflect new jurisprudence and other significant developments. It serves as a complement to the Third Edition of the WTO Analytical Index, and it should be read in conjunction with the Third Edition. It also serves as a useful, self-contained guide for readers interested in the most recent developments in WTO law and practice.

WTO distance learning:

https://www.wto.org/english/res_e/d_learn_e/d_learn_e.htm

The WTO offers on this page a number of interactive training modules on WTO subjects. Each module is built on course material developed by WTO experts and includes a number of interactive tests to assess the user's progress.

WTO Statistics Database:

http://stat.wto.org/Home/WSDBHome.aspx?Language=E

The WTO Statistics Database allows you to retrieve statistical information in the following presentations:

- The Trade Profiles provide predefined information leaflets on the trade situation of Members, observers and other selected economies;
- The Tariff Profiles provide information on the market access situation of Members, observers and other selected economies;
- The Services Profiles provide detailed statistics on key infrastructure services (transportation, telecommunications, finance and insurance) for selected economies;

- The Aid for Trade Profiles provide information on trends of aid for trade, trade costs, trade performance and development for selected Aid for Trade recipients;
- The Time Series section allows an interactive data retrieval of international trade statistics.

causation, 119–120, 150–151
CITES. *See* Convention on
 International Trade in
 Endangered Species
Code of Good Practice, 179–180
COMESA. *See* Common Market
 of Eastern and Southern
 Africa
commercial presence mode of
 supply, 25–26
Committee on Balance-of-
 Payments Restrictions (BoP
 Committee), 127–128
Committee on Regional Trade
 Agreements, 243–244
Committee on Regional Trade
 Agreements (or the
 Committee on Trade and
 Development), 135
Committee on Subsidies and
 Countervailing Measures,
 243–244
Committee on Trade and
 Development, 243–244
Committee on Trade and
 Environment, 243–244
Common Market of Eastern and
 Southern Africa
 (COMESA), 129–131
Common Market of the Caribbean
 (CARICOM), 129–131
compensation, 125
compliance dispute, 286
compulsory licences, 226, 227
confidentiality, 290–292
conformity assessment procedures,
 179–180, 188–189

consensus, 255–256, 261–262,
 270–272
constructive remedies, 155
consultations, 274–277
consumption abroad mode of
 supply, 24–25
Convention on Biological
 Diversity, 9
Convention on International Trade
 in Endangered Species
 (CITES), 9
copyright, 214, 215–216, 221–222, 224
Cotton-Four. *See* Member country
 groupings
Council for Trade in Goods (CTG),
 243–244
Council for Trade in Services
 (CTS), 80, 243–244
Council for Trade Related Aspects
 of Intellectual Property
 Rights. *See* TRIPS Council
countervailing investigations. *See*
 SCM Agreement
countervailing measures, 158,
 170–173. *See also* SCM
 Agreement
covered agreements, 259–260,
 265–266
cross appeal, 281–282
cross border mode of supply,
 24–25
CTG. *See* Council for Trade in
 Goods
CTS. *See* Council for Trade in
 Services
customs classification, 55–56
customs duties. *See* tariffs